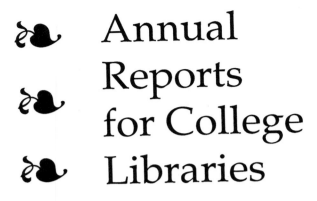

Annual Reports for College Libraries

CLIP Note #10

Compiled by

Kenneth J. Oberembt

Director, Alumni Memorial Library
University of Scranton, Pennsylvania

College Library Information Packet Committee
College Libraries Section
Association of College and Research Libraries
a division of the American Library Association

Published by the Association of College and
Research Libraries, a division of the
American Library Association
50 East Huron Street
Chicago, Illinois 60611

ISBN 0-8389-7219-5

The paper used in this publication meets the minimum
requirements of American National Standard for
Information Sciences--Permanence of Paper for Printed
Library Materials, ANSI Z39.48-1984. ♾

Printed in the United States of America.

TABLE OF CONTENTS

INTRODUCTION

Objective:

The College Library Information Packet Note publishing program, under the auspices of the College Libraries Section of the Association of College & Research Libraries, provides "college and small university libraries with state-of-the-art reviews and current documentation on library practices and procedures of relevance to them." This CLIP Note offers some ideas for developing or redeveloping the annual report document and encourages its use in strengthening client support for the library.

Background:

When Mark Nesse wrote that public librarians often look upon the annual report as a "nuisance," he could just as easily have had academic librarians in mind. For both, the annual report exercise is frequently a requirement, the process of amassing information time-consuming, and the editing of the final product draining. Even if they wonder whether the annual report is ever read by decision-makers outside of the library, librarians might well agree with Nesse that the annual report can be useful when it tries "to inform the public of the value of library services" and to be a "vehicle for the discussion of library problems and potentials." And they might, additionally, justify its usefulness as a compendium of statistics easily mined for answers to legitimate queries and as an historical source for documenting library activities.

The library annual report may be bound by rigorous institutional requirements or follow the fancy of a whimsical director, be brief or lengthy, be focused or diffuse, be addressed to an audience of one or thousands, be pertinent or pointless. Taken out of its local context, it is hard to judge how effective it really is. What is certain is that library annual reports have always been written (so it seems) and will continue to be written. If we can't avoid doing them, then we owe it to ourselves to make them as useful to the library as possible. And that is the reason for this CLIP Note publication.

Survey Procedure:

The procedure followed was the standard one for CLIP Note projects. A proposal and questionnaire were drafted for review by the CLIP Note Committee of ACRL's College Libraries Section. The revised questionnaire was later distributed (October 1987) to 191 libraries that had made a prior commitment to participate in CLIP Note surveys. These libraries represent a selection from two groups outlined in the Carnegie Council on Policy Studies in Higher Education (1976): Comprehensive Universities and Colleges I, and Liberal Arts Colleges I. The survey group was asked to return with the completed questionnaire copies of recent annual reports, data and information gathering forms used in the preparation of annual reports, and any annual report variants prepared for different audiences. Questionnaire responses were compiled by means of The Statistical Package for the Social Sciences (SPSS) software and the documents enclosed with the questionnaires evaluated and selected for the present publication.

Survey Results:

CLIP Note publications emphasize documents that highlight current library practice and procedure; information elicited by questionnaire is meant only to provide a statistical and valuational backdrop for the documents.

The 191 libraries solicited returned 128 questionnaires (67.0%), 117 (61.3%) usable, by the November 1987 deadline date. Apart from demographic and fiscal information specific to the institution, each library was asked whether or not it prepared an annual report. If so, how it was prepared, structured, produced, distributed, and valued; if not, why not and what alternatives to annual reporting were in use.

Preparation of annual reports (B.8.a, C.9 - 11).

Of the responding libraries, 81 (69.2%) regularly prepare annual reports. Cross tabulation with demographic and fiscal data shows no significant difference between libraries with and libraries without an annual reporting procedure. Size of FTE student enrollment, FTE library staff, and annual library expenditures are similar across the two groups.

By an overwhelming margin, 52 (64.2%) as against 29 (35.8%), libraries observe a requirement of their parent institutions to submit annual reports. By and large it is the library director who manages the drafting and final editing tasks. Other library administrators, librarians, and library support staff influence the final product chiefly by contributing information to be included in it. Library advisory committees, faculty, and students (including student workers in the library) play little or no role in annual report preparation.

Structure of annual reports (D.12 - 14).

The topics addressed by 50% or more of the 81 libraries in their annual reports are, in descending order of importance: 1. collection growth and usage (78); 2. operations by department or function, usage of public services (tie--74); 4. budget/expenditures (62); 5. physical facilities, future needs (tie--58); 7. annual goals and objectives (53); and 8. library consortia (45). The choice of annual report topics is either the responsibility of the directors and their associate or assistant directors (47.0%) or a collaborate decision of the forementioned and department heads (28.9%). Three quarters (76.3%) of the respondents use a consistent annual report structure from year to year; only one library acknowledged significant variation from one year to the next.

Production of annual reports (E.15 - 18).

Of the 81 libraries, 50 (61.7%) record the length of the most recent edition as exceeding 10 pages. Within this group 17 (21.0%) report a size of 26 pages or more. The favored method of duplication, numbering 51 (63.8%) of respondents, is photocopy equipment sited in the library. A review of the documents enclosed with the questionnaire reveals that libraries are not yet making use of computer desktop publishing equipment to produce their master copy. The typical annual report is a stand-alone publication with a total print run of 50 copies or less. Editions beyond 100 copies (9 libraries) are atypical.

Distribution of annual reports (F.19 - 20).

Only 24 (22.0%) of the 81 libraries disseminate their annual reports as handouts strategically placed within the library building or around the college campus. Given that so few duplicate their report documents in more than 50 copies, it is not certain that the handout is in all instances actually "public." The primary recipients are, in order of rank: 1. chief academic officer (71); 2. president (56); and 3. librarians (48). No other campus constituency was on the mailing lists of even half of the respondents.

Value of annual reports (G.21 - 25).

The raison d'etre of annual reports, in the judgment of those who prepare them, is 1. to publicize library achievements; 2. to explain future library needs; 3. to justify continued financial support; 4. to maintain a public presence for the library; 5. to make a case for special funding; and 6. to fulfill an administrative requirement, in that order. The annual report is also judged to be "very important" to library management, "important" to the college administration and library non-managerial staff, and "not important" to patrons.

Libraries without annual reports (B.8.b, H.27).

In the group of 117 libraries responding to the CLIP Note survey, 36 (30.8%) do not engage in an annual report exercise. They rely on alternative reporting mechanisms, chiefly meetings with and memoranda to the institutional officer or board with oversight responsibility for the library. Only one respondent hinted at impending development of a formal annual report document. The main reason, however, for not doing a library annual report is simply that the college administration does not require one, a situation with which several respondents professed to be well satisfied.

Annual report documents:

In response to the CLIP Note survey, libraries sent 69 copies of their most recent annual reports--approximately 1,500 pages worth of material. Therefore rigorous selection was necessary. Included in this publication are

1. short annual report documents showing compilers at their best in selecting out of the great mass of activities during the year those that best tell the library story,

2. annual reports with special graphic features that make the final product visually attractive or illuminate the narrative, and

3. report documents targeted at an audience of library patrons, usually with print runs in excess of 50 copies.

In addition to five complete annual report documents, this publication also includes sections for annual report data-gathering forms and annual report graphics (a selection).

WORKS CITED

Morein, P. Grady. "What is a CLIP Note?" *College and ResearchLibraries News* 46 (1985): 226.

Nesse, Mark A. "Annual Reports with Punch." *Public Libraries* (Summer 1980): 46.

CLIP NOTES SURVEY
THE LIBRARY ANNUAL REPORT

THIS SURVEY DOCUMENT IS DESIGNED TO GATHER INFORMATION ABOUT THE ACADEMIC LIBRARY ANNUAL REPORT--ITS PREPARATION, STRUCTURE, PRODUCTION, DISTRIBUTION, AND VALUE TO THE LIBRARY.

THANK YOU IN ADVANCE FOR YOUR RESPONSE.

A. GENERAL INFORMATION.

1) Name of respondent: _____

2) Position title: _____

3) Institution: _____

4) Address: _____

_____

5) Approximate full-time equivalent (FTE) student enrollment at your institution (Fall 1987):

_____

113 Responses: Range 400 - 6240; Mean 2623.0; Median 2243.0

6) Number of full-time equivalent (FTE) library staff at your institution (Fall 1987):

_____

112 Responses: Range 3.5 - 73.0; Mean 20.7; Median 18.0

7) Approximate total operating budget of your library for fiscal year 1987-1988:

_____

109 Responses: Range 64999 - 2809140; Mean 882975; Median 720000

B. ANNUAL REPORT INFORMATION: GENERAL

8) Does your library prepare an annual end-of-the academic or fiscal year report?

117 Responses

a) *81* Yes (complete questions 9 - 26 below and <u>send a copy of your most recent annual report</u> with this completed questionnaire)

b) *36* No (go to question 27 below)

C. ANNUAL REPORT INFORMATION: PREPARATION

9) Is submission of a library annual report required or voluntary at your institution?

   81 Responses

   a) _52_ Required

   b) _29_ Voluntary

10) Were standard data-gathering forms used to collect information for your most recent library annual report?

   78 Responses

   a) _22_ Yes (please <u>return sample copies</u> with this completed questionnaire)

   b) _56_ No

11) Who was involved in the preparation of your most recent library annual report? (Check <u>all</u> that apply)

   81 Responses

Edit(s) Report   Draft(s) Text   Contribute(s) Information

a1) _73_	a2) _74_	a3) _62_	Library Director
b1) _11_	b2) _14_	b3) _32_	Asst/Assoc Director(s)
c1) _7_	c2) _22_	c3) _61_	Dept/Division Heads
d1) _5_	d2) _15_	d3) _65_	Librarians/Professionals
e1) _5_	e2) _5_	e3) _46_	Non-Professional Staff
f1) _0_	f2) _0_	f3) _1_	Student Workers
g1) _0_	g2) _1_	g3) _4_	Library Advisory Committee
h1) _0_	h2) _0_	h3) _2_	Faculty
i1) _0_	i2) _0_	i3) _2_	Students
j1) _3_	j2) _3_	j3) _2_	Other (specify)

Administrative Assistant

12) Which of the following topics was addressed in your most recent library annual report? (Check <u>all</u> that apply)

81 Responses

a) _10_ Mission Statement of the institution

b) _17_ Long-Range Plan of the institution

c) _14_ ACRL Standards for College Libraries

d) _22_ Mission Statement of the library

e) _12_ Library accreditation/reaccreditation

f) _39_ Long-Range Plan of the library

g) _53_ Annual goals and objectives of the library

h) _74_ Library operations (by department or function)

i) _62_ Library budget/expenditures

j) _58_ Library physical facilities

k) _78_ Library collection growth and usage

l) _74_ Usage of library public services

m)_45_ Consortia in which the library holds membership

n) _21_ Library Friends organization

o) _58_ Future needs of the library

p) _11_ Other (specify)

    10   Library personnel (professional activities, turnover, evaluation of, additional needs)

    2   Library automation and computer-based services

    1   Library advisory/oversight committee

    1   Library gifts

13) Who selected the topics to be covered in your most recent library annual report?

81 Responses

a) *3* Specified by the college/university administration

b) *39* Selected by the Library Director/Asst and/or Assoc Director(s)

c) *1* Selected by library department/division heads

d) *9* Combination of a) and b)

e) *24* Combination of b) and c)

f) *5* Combination of a), b), and c)

g) *2* Other (specify)

      1   *Guided by HEGIS requirements*

      1   *Library support staff*

14) Does your library annual report use a standard structure from year to year?

80 Responses

a) *61* A basically consistent structure

b) *18* Structure varies somewhat from year to year

c) *1* Structure varies considerably from year to year

E. ANNUAL REPORT INFORMATION: PRODUCTION

15) What was the number of pages in your most recent library annual report?

81 Responses

a) *10* 1 - 5 pages

b) *21* 6 - 10 pages

c) *33* 11 - 25 pages

d) *17* 26+ pages

8

6) What method of production was used for your most recent library annual report? (Check all that apply)

80 Responses

a) _51_ Duplicated on library equipment

b) _24_ Printed by the institutional print shop

c) _1_ Printed commercially

d) _4_ Other (specify)

    1   *Duplicated by the secretarial services unit*

    2   *Typewritten (single copy publication)*

    1   *Duplication by the institution's copy center*

7) What type of publication was used for your most recent library annual report? (Check all that apply and send copies of variant versions with this completed questionnaire.)

79 Responses

a) _68_ Published as a separate document

b) _0_ Included in an issue of the newsletter to library users

c) _1_ Included in the newsletter to library staff

d) _0_ Included in an issue of the institutional newsletter to faculty/staff

e) _0_ Included in an issue of the student newspaper

f) _17_ Incorporated into the President's annual report

g) _4_ Other (specify)

    1   *Included in a bimonthly library newsletter to faculty*

    1   *Included in the chief academic officer's annual report*

    1   *Included in an institutional campuswide newsletter*

    1   *Included in a highlights-of-the-month library report to library staff*

18) What was the number of published copies of your most recent library annual report?

80 Responses

a) _33_ 1 - 10

b) _32_ 11 - 50

c) _6_ 51 - 100

d) _5_ 10I - 250

e) _4_ 251 - 500

f) _0_ 501 - 1,000

g) _0_ Above 1,000

F. ANNUAL REPORT INFORMATION: DISTRIBUTION

19) What was the method of distribution for your most recent library annual report? (Check <u>all</u> that apply)

76 Responses

a) _66_ Campus mail

b) _18_ Handout available within the library

c) _6_ Handout strategically placed around campus

d) _0_ Electronic mail

e) _12_ U.S.P.S.

f) _7_ Other (specify)

    1 Distributed by University Relations Office as PR

    2 Placed on library reserve

    3 Hand delivered

    1 Distributed by multi-college mail service

    1 Placed in University Archives

) To whom was your most recent library annual report distributed? (Check <u>all</u> that apply)

81 Responses

a) *17* Board of Trustees

b) *56* President

c) *71* Chief Academic Officer

d) *31* Vice Presidents

e) *31* Deans

f) *17* Directors of other units on campus

g) *4* College/University Senate

h) *6* New or prospective employees

i) *20* Library managers

j) *48* Librarians/Professionals

k) *34* Total library staff

l) *34* Library Advisory Committee

m) *7* Faculty

n) *0* Students

o) *5* Friends Group

p) *1* Donors/prospective donors

q) *13* Consortia member libraries

r) *15* Other (specify)

    1   *Chairs/heads of academic departments*

    1   *Available on library reserve*

    4   *Sent in fulfillment of a request*

    2   *Institutional alumni*

    4   *Selected libraries*

    1   *President of the student senate*

    1   *Editor of the student newspaper*

G. ANNUAL REPORT INFORMATION: VALUE

21) How is the library annual report used by your library at your institution?
(Rank each item on a scale of 5 - 1: 5 = Very Important, 1 = Not Important)

a) _____ To publicize library achievements

64 Responses: 37 ranked "5 = Very Important"; Mean 4.063

b) _____ To generate/maintain user support

57 Responses: 8 ranked "5 = Very Important"; Mean 2.561

c) _____ To make a case for special funding

58 Responses: 13 ranked "5 = Very Important"; Mean 3.241

d) _____ To describe national library trends

52 Responses: 1 ranked "5 = Very Important"; Mean 2.115

e) _____ To justify continued financial support

60 Responses: 26 ranked "5 = Very Important"; Mean 3.733

f) _____ To solicit external funds

52 Responses: 2 ranked "5 = Very Important"; Mean 1.865

g) _____ To explain the future needs of the library

62 Responses: 24 ranked "5 = Very Important"; Mean 3.968

h) _____ To maintain a public presence for the library

58 Responses: 15 ranked "5 = Very Important"; Mean 3.293

i) _____ To fulfill an administrative requirement to publish
information about the library

56 Responses: 24 ranked "5 = Very Important"; Mean 3.196

j) _____ To emulate the annual report publications of other campus units

52 Responses: 3 ranked "5 = Very Important"; Mean 1.731

k) _____ Other (specify)

10 Responses: 8 ranked "5 = Very Important"; Mean 4.600

   5   *To create a convenient historical source document*

   5   *To keep the college and library administration informed and educated on library affairs*

   2   *To enhance staff involvement in the library*

   1   *To facilitate planning*

22) How important is your Library annual report to the library administration?
(Circle the response that best reflects your judgment)

Very Important   Not Important   No Opinion

    5 · 4 3   2 1   0

81 Responses: 39 ranked "5 = Very Important"; Mean 4.160

23) How important is your library annual report to library staff?
(Circle the response that best reflects your judgment)

Very Important   Not Important   No Opinion

    5   4 3   2 1   0

81 Responses: 7 ranked "5 = Very Important"; Mean 3.259

24) How important is your library annual report to your college/university administration?
(Circle the response that best reflects your judgment)

Very Important   Not Important   No Opinion

    5   4 3   2 1   0

81 Responses: 20 ranked "5 = Very Important"; Mean 3.667

25) How important is your library annual report to your library users?
(Circle the response that best reflects your judgment)

Very Important   Not Important   No Opinion

    5   4 3   2 1   0

81 Responses: 1 ranked "5 = Very Important"; Mean 1.333

26) Permission to publish documents (check <u>one</u> of the following).

_____ I give permission to publish in a <u>CLIP Notes</u> publication any documents I send with this completed questionnaire.

_____ Permission to publish in a <u>CLIP Notes</u> publication any documents I send with this completed questionnaire requires this copyright statement:

_____

_____

IF YOU ANSWERED <u>YES</u> TO QUESTION 8 ABOVE, YOU HAVE NOW COMPLETED THE SURVEY. PLEASE RETURN YOUR COMPLETED QUESTIONNAIRE WITH COPIES OF YOUR ANNUAL REPORT DOCUMENT(S) AND ANNUAL REPORT DATA-GATHERING FORMS. USE THE ENCLOSED MAILING LABEL. THANK YOU.

H. ANNUAL REPORT INFORMATION: LIBRARIES WITHOUT ANNUAL REPORTS

27) Indicate the reason(s) why your library does not prepare an annual report document. (Rank each item on a scale of 5 - 1: 5 = Very Important, 1 = Not Important)

a) _____ Not required by the college/university administration

23 Responses: 16 ranked "5 = Very Important"; Mean 4.391

b) _____ Use another kind of report mechanism (specify)

11 Periodic oral or written reports to oversight academic officer or board

3 Library newsletter articles

2 Budget submission document

2 Memoranda

2 Strategic plan document

1 Reaccreditation report

1 Annual statistical report

1 Regular reports from library department heads

1 Regular reports to the institutional news bureau

23 Responses: 4 ranked "5 = Very Important"; Mean 3.043

c) _____ Not useful to the library in retaining support and resources

18 Responses: 3 ranked "5 = Very Important"; Mean 2.944

d) _____ Inferior to other records maintained by the library to keep library administration and staff abreast of developments

19 Responses: 2 ranked "5 = Very Important"; Mean 2.842

e) _____ Not a useful information document for library users

17 Responses: 3 ranked "5 = Very Important"; Mean 2.412

f) _____ Unimportant for solicitation of external funds

16 Responses: 4 ranked "5 = Very Important"; Mean 2.500

g) _____ Too much work for too few results

20 Responses: 7 ranked "5 = Very Important"; Mean 3.450

h) _____ Other (specify)

    2   *Too great a burden for an understaffed library*

    1   *HEGIS report serves just as well*

    1   *Problem of consistent statistics*

    1   *No real impact on institutional decision makers*

5 Responses: 3 ranked "5 = Very Important"; Mean 4.200

IF YOU ANSWERED <u>NO</u> TO QUESTION 8 AND ALSO ANSWERED QUESTION 27, YOU HAVE COMPLETED THE SURVEY. RETURN YOUR COMPLETED QUESTIONNAIRE. USE THE ENCLOSED MAILING LABEL. THANK YOU.

DATA-GATHERING FORMS

SELECTED STATISTICS

19   -

1. Collection - financial
   - Books _____
   - Books endowed _____
   - Books gift _____
   - Black Studies _____
   - total _____
   - HEW grant _____
   - total _____
   - Periodicals _____
   - total _____
   - Microtext _____
   - total _____
   - Discs _____
   - total _____
   - Binding _____
   - total _____
   - Other _____
   - total _____

   (Number of books paid for _____)
   Average book cost   _____

   (Number of subs paid for _____)
   Average sub cost   _____

   (Total ed. & gen. expense _____
   Library % with fringes _____
           without _____

   Total Library expend.   _____

   Rpt. for Title II   _____

   : _____

II. Collection - development (as of 30 June, 19   .)

	Totals		Added	
Books, vol.	_____	(titles____; vol. _____	_____	(titles_____)
Bound periods.	_____	(no. of subs____;	_____	(no. of subs_____
Micro	_____		_____	
Discs	_____		_____	
Docs	_____		_____	

III. Acquisitions and cataloging
   - Book orders received _____
   - Duplicate orders _____ (%____)
   - Orders from staff _____ (%____)
   - % in data base _____
   - % not searched _____

   Missing since last Inventory:

   Received: vols._____ (titles_____
   Gifts: vols._____ (titles_____
   Cataloged: vols._____ (titles_____
   Withdrawn: vols._____ (titles_____
   Reclassed: vols._____ (titles_____
   vols._____ (titles_____

IV. Staffing
   - Prof. salaries _____
   - Full time salaries _____
   - Part time salaries _____
   - T/T salaries _____
   - Other salaries _____
   - (from comptroller) _____
   - Total staff salaries _____
   - Total fringe benefits _____
   - Total staff costs _____

   (Student hours_____)
   Student wages_____

   Total personnel costs _____

V. Circulation

	Student	Total
Book	_____	_____
Periodicals	_____	_____
Docs. etc.	_____	_____
Reserve	_____	_____
Discs	_____	_____

   ILL: borrowed _____
         loaned   _____

   Photocopy: requested_____
           filled   _____

READER SERVICES STATISTICS

Period covered:

REFERENCE TRANSACTIONS:

	JUL	AUG	SEP	OCT	NOV	DEC	JAN	FEB	MAR	APR	MAY	JUN	TOTAL
Last year:													
This year:													

% CHANGE:

DATABASE SEARCHES:

	JUL	AUG	SEP	OCT	NOV	DEC	JAN	FEB	MAR	APR	MAY	JUN	TOTAL
Last year:													
This year:													

% CHANGE:

Cost of searches: Average cost/search:
  Last year: Last year:
  This year: % change: This year: % change:

Searches this year for Faculty: Staff: Students: Other:

BIBLIOGRAPHIC INSTRUCTION/LIBRARY ORIENTATION TRANSACTIONS:

Effective Writing: Sections taught (5 hours ea.)   Students taught

        Last year:
        This year:

Other instruction: Classes taught   Students taught

        Last year:
        This year:

Orientation/instruction for outside groups: # of groups   # of people

        Last year:
        This year:

CIRCULATION TRANSACTIONS:

	JUL	AUG	SEP	OCT	NOV	DEC	JAN	FEB	MAR	APR	MAY	JUN	TOTAL
NONRESERVE ITEMS													
Last year:													
This year:													
RESERVE ITEMS													
Last year:													
This year:													
ALL ITEMS													
Last year:													
This year:													

% change, all items: Active Town Patron cards:
                                         (as of 30 June)

Total circulation to Students: Faculty/Staff: Town Patrons:
                                  ILL: Other Schools (direct loans):

INTERLIBRARY LOAN TRANSACTIONS:

	JUL	AUG	SEP	OCT	NOV	DEC	JAN	FEB	MAR	APR	MAY	JUN	TOTAL
ITEMS BORROWED													
Last year:													
This year:													
% change:													
ITEMS LOANED													
Last year:													
This year:													
% change:													

TOTAL ITEMS PROCESSED LAST YEAR: THIS YEAR: % CHANGE:

Ratio of items borrowed to items lent:

LIBRARY COLLECTIONS

TYPE OF RESOURCES	HELD PREV. YEAR	ADDED	WITHDRAWN AND/OR LOST & PAID	RE-INSTATED	MISSING	HELD END OF YEAR
PRINTED MATERIALS						
Traditional Print						
Books						
Bound Periodicals						
Total Hard Copy						
Micro-Reproductions						
Microcards						
Microfiche						
Microfilm						
Total Micro-Reproductions						
GRAND TOTAL PRINTED						
NON-PRINT MATERIALS						
Films						
Film Loops						
Films (8mm)						
Films (16mm)						
Filmstrips						
Filmstrips w/sound						
Recordings						
Audio Tapes						
Disc Records (33 1/3)						
Tape Cassettes						
Video Tapes						
Miscellaneous						
Globes						
Pictures/Prints						
Slides						
Slides w/sound						
Transparencies						
Wall Maps						
Kits						
GRAND TOTAL NON-PRINTED						

LYNCHBURG COLLEGE LIBRARY

Circulation Statistics

MONTH	BOOKS	MEDIA	TOTAL
July			
August			
September			
October			
November			
December			
January			
February			
March			
April			
May			
June			
TOTAL			

LYNCHBURG COLLEGE LIBRARY

STATISTICAL REPORT

INTERLIBRARY LOANS

| MONTH | INCOMING LOANS | | OUTGOING LOANS | | TOTAL TRANSACTIONS |
	Requests Made	Requests Filled	Requests Made	Requests Filled	
July					
August					
September					
October					
November					
December					
January					
February					
March					
April					
May					
June					
TOTAL					

LYNCHBURG COLLEGE LIBRARY STATISTICS

ass/Dept.	Books	T	Serials	T	Discard	Lost in Circ.	Lost in Invent.	Rein-state	TOTAL ADDED
GENERAL									
PHILOSOPHY									
PSYCHOLOGY									
PHILOSOPHY									
RELIGION									
HISTORY									
BIOLOGY									
SOCIOLOGY									
HEALTH, P.E.									
SOCIOLOGY									
ECONOMICS									
BUSINESS									
SOCIOLOGY									
POL. SCI.									
POL. SCI.									
EDUCATION									
MUSIC									
ART									
FORN. LANG.									
ENGLISH									
FORN.LANG.									
59 ENGLISH									
-3299 DRAMA									
-7000 ENGLISH									
FORN. LANG.									
ENGLISH									
FORN. LANG.									
ENGLISH									
BIOLOGY									
MATH									
COMPUTER SCI.									
99 MATH									
PHYSICS									
CHEMISTRY									
BIOLOGY									
NURSING									
NURSING									
BIOLOGY									
PHYSICS									
CHEMISTRY									
BUSINESS									
ART									
GENERAL									
HISTORY									
GENERAL									
EDUCATION									
ROOM									
BLICATIONS									
ES OF CHRIST									
ANEOUS									
S:									

SWARTHMORE COLLEGE LIBRARY

STATISTICS

		June 198	Added	Withdrawals	Jun
1	BOOKS, PERIODICALS (vols)				
2	DOCUMENTS (total 3 & 4)				
3	U.S.				
4	Pennsylvania				
5	TOTAL (1 + 2)				
6	Microfilm Reels				
7	Microfiche (units)				
8	MICROPRINT				
9	MAPS, CHARTS, etc.				
10	AUDIOVISUAL MATERIALS				
11	Videocassettes				
12	Phonograph Records (13 - 15)				
13	Auden Collection				
14	Potter Poetry				
15	Swarthmoreana				
16	CASSETTE RECORDINGS (17-20)				
17	General				
18	Auden				
19	Potter				
20	Swarthmoreana				
21	PERIODICAL SUBSCRIPTIONS				
22	CORNELL SCIENCE LIBRARY				
23	UNDERHILL MUSIC LIBRARY				
24	Books, Periodicals (vols.)				
25	Recordings				
26	CIRCULATION (27-28)				
27	General				
28	Reserve				
29	INTERLIBRARY LOANS				
30	Books Borrowed				
31	Books Loaned				
32	Photocopies received				
33	Photocopies sent				

MJD:asb
8/85

	MC CABE	CORNELL	OBSERVATORY	MUSIC	REFERENCE	CLOSED ST.	TREASURE RM.	AUDEN	BATHE	BRITISH AM.	BROADSIDES	PR. PRESS	SWARTHMOREANA	WELLS	TOTAL
icals															
ings															
c															
e															
sette															
assettes															
ilm															
iche															
ard															
A L															

I. Monographs
   A. Titles
      Main Library _____

      Swarthmoreana _____
      Private Press _____
      Treasure Room _____
      Auden Collection _____
      British Americana _____
      Bathe Collection _____

      Cornell _____
      Observatory _____
      Music (books) _____
      Music (scores) _____
                                                        Total titles
   B. Volumes
      Main Library _____

      Swarthmoreana _____
      Private Press _____
      Treasure Room _____
      Auden Collection _____
      British Americana _____
      Bathe Collection _____

      Cornell _____
      Observatory _____
      Music (books) _____
      Music (scores) _____
                                                        Total volumes

II. Serials
   A. Titles
      1. Periodicals
         Main Library _____
         Cornell _____
         Observatory _____
         Music _____
                                                        Total titles
      2. Continuations
         Main Library _____
         Cornell _____
         Observatory _____
         Music _____
                                                        Total titles
   B. Volumes
      1. Periodicals
         Main Library _____
         Cornell _____
         Observatory _____
         Music _____
                                                        Total volumes
      2. Continuations
         Main Library _____
         Cornell _____
         Observatory _____
         Music _____
                                                        Total volumes

ACQUISITION FUNDS

	Monographs	Periodicals	Continuations	TOTAL
HUMANITIES				
Art				
Classics				
English				
Modern Languages				
French				
German				
Russian				
Spanish				
Other				
Music				
Philosophy				
Religion				
NATURAL SCIENCES				
Astronomy				
Biology				
Chemistry				
Engineering				
Mathematics				
Physics				
SOCIAL SCIENCES				
Economics				
Education				
History				
Linguistics				
Political Science				
Psychology				
Sociology/Anthropology				
LIBRARY				
Humanities				
Natural Sciences				
Social Sciences				
Contingency				
General				
TOTAL BOOKS				
AUDIOVISUALS				
McCabe				
Music				
Science				

LIBRARY/MEDIA RESOURCES CENTER STATISTICS

A. CURRENT HOLDINGS

Books and Periodicals

_____ 1. Books (number of volumes)

_____ 2. Books (number of titles)

_____ 3. Bound periodicals (number of volumes)

_____ 4. Total of book and periodical volumes (A1 and 3)

Print Media

_____ 5. Microfilm (number of reels)

_____ 6. Microfiche (number of pieces)

_____ 7. Microcards (number of pieces)

_____ 8. Total of microforms (A5 through 7)

_____ 9. Total microform volume-equivalents (A5 and [A6 and 7 divided

Non-Print Media
(number of pieces unless otherwise specified)

_____ 10. Slides

_____ 11. Video cassettes, video tapes, video discs

_____ 12. Films

_____ 13. Film strips, including sound film strips

_____ 14. Film loops

_____ 15. Transparencies

_____ 16. Mixed media sets (number of sets)

_____ 17. Total of visual non-print items (A10 through 16)

_____ 18. Phonodiscs

_____ 19. Audio tapes and cassettes

_____ 20. Total of sound recordings (A18 and 19)

_____ 21. Computer-based educational software

_____ 22. Grand total of non-print items (A17, 20, and 21)

B. ANNUAL GROWTH OF THE COLLECTIONS

Books and Periodicals

_____ 1. Books added by purchase (number of volumes)

_____ 2. Books added by purchase (number of titles)

_____ 3. Books added by gift (number of volumes)

_____ 4. Books added by gift (number of titles)

_____ 5. Total of book volumes added (B1 and 3)

_____ 6. Total of book titles added (B2 and 4)

_____ 7. Bound periodicals added (number of volumes)

_____ 8. Total of book and bound periodical volumes added (B5 and 7)

_____ 9. Volumes withdrawn (number of book volumes)

_____ 10. Volumes withdrawn (number of periodical volumes)

_____ 11. Net gain in volumes (B8 minus 9 and 10)

Print Media

_____ 12. Microfilm added (number of reels)

_____ 13. Microfiche added (number of pieces)

_____ 14. Microcards added (number of pieces)

_____ 15. Total of microforms added (B12 through 14)

_____ 16. Microforms withdrawn (number of reels and pieces)

_____ 17. Net gain in microforms (B15 minus 16)

_____ 18. Net gain in microform volume-equivalents (B12 and [B13 and 14
divided by 5])

Non-Print Media
(number of pieces unless otherwise specified)

_____ 19. Slides added

_____ 20. Video cassettes, video tapes, video discs added

_____ 21. Films added

_____ 22. Film strips added, including sound film strips

_____ 23. Film loops added

_____ 24. Transparencies added

_____ 25. Mixed media sets added (number of sets)

_____ 26. Total of visual non-print items added (B19 through 25)

_____ 27. Phonodiscs added

_____ 28. Audio tapes and cassettes added

_____ 29. Total of sound recordings added (B27 and 28)

_____ 30. Computer-based educational software added

_____ 31. Grand total of non-print items added (B26, 29, and 30)

_____ 32. Total withdrawals of non-print items

_____ 33. Net gain in non-print items (B31 minus 32)

C. SUBSCRIPTIONS

_____ 1. Paid periodical titles

_____ 2. Gift periodical titles

_____ 3. New periodical titles added during the year

_____ 4. Total of periodical titles (C1 and 2)

_____ 5. Paid serial titles

_____ 6. Gift serial titles

_____ 7. New serial titles added during the year

_____ 8. Total of serial titles (C5 and 6)

_____ 9. Total microform subscriptions, standing orders and information services (number of titles)

10. Total microform subscriptions for

    a. Periodicals (number of titles) _____

    b. Serials, standing orders, information services (number of titles) _____

_____ 11. Microform subscriptions, standing orders, and information services added during the year (number of titles)

12. New microform subscriptions for

    a. Periodicals (number of titles) _____

    b. Serials, standing orders, information services (number of titles) _____

UNIVERSITY OF SCRANTON LIBRARY

D. SERVICES

Circulation: Books and Periodicals

_____ 1. Number of circulating collection volumes charged out

_____ 2. Number of reserved materials charged out

_____ 3. Reshelving count of number of items used in-house

_____ 4. Total circulation of print-based materials (D1 through 3)

_____ 5. Hold notices

_____ 6. Overdue notices (first notice, second notice)

_____ 7. Bills for replacement costs and associated charges

_____ 8. Bills for unpaid fines

Circulation: Print Media

_____ 9. Reshelving count of number of microforms (reels and pieces used in-house)

Circulation: Non-Print Media

_____ 10. Number of reserved materials charged out for use in classrooms, at mediated carrels, and in the preview rooms

_____ 11. Total circulations of print and non-print reserved materials (D2 and 10)

_____ 12. Grand total of circulations of print and non-print materials (D4, 9, and 10)

Interlibrary Loan: Books and Periodicals

_____ 13. Number of books borrowed

_____ 14. Number of photoprints received

_____ 15. Total number of interlibrary loans acquired (D13 and 14)

_____ 16. Number of interlibrary loans borrowed or received from NEPBC libraries

17. Total number of requests filled for

    a. University faculty _____

    b. University graduate students _____

    c. University undergraduate students _____

    d. Other _____

18. Total number of sources located through

    a. NEPBC   _____

    b. OCLC   _____

    c. Other   _____

_____ 19. Number of books loaned

_____ 20. Number of photoprints supplied

_____ 21. Total number of interlibrary loans provided (D19 and 20)

_____ 22. Number of interlibrary loans supplied to NEPBC libraries

23. Total number of outgoing items shipped via

    a. Local Delivery Service   _____

    b. IDS   _____

    c. Mail   _____

    d. Other   _____

Interlibrary Loan: Non-Print Media

_____ 24. Number of media items borrowed, including rentals, from other institutions

25. Number of media items borrowed, including rentals, for

    a. Biology Department   _____

    b. Chemistry Department   _____

    c. Communications Department   _____

    d. Dexter Hanley College   _____

    e. Education Department   _____

    f. English Department   _____

    g. Fine Arts Department   _____

    h. Foreign Languages Department   _____

    i. History/Political Science Department   _____

    j. Human Resources Department   _____

    k. Mathematics/Computer Science Department   _____

l. Military Science Department _____

m. Nursing Department _____

n. Philosophy Department _____

o. Physical Education Department _____

p. Physical Therapy Department _____

q. Physics Department _____

r. Psychology Department _____

s. School of Management _____

t. Sociology/Criminal Justice/
   Gerontology Department _____

u. Theology/Religious Studies Department _____

v. Other _____

_____ 26. Number of media items borrowed from NEPBC institutions

_____ 27. Number of media items loaned to other institutions

_____ 28. Grand total of interlibrary loan receipts (D 15 and 24)

_____ 29. Grand total of interlibrary loans supplied (D21 and 27)

Reference Services

_____ 30. Reference questions per typical week

_____ 31. Directional questions per typical week

_____ 32. Total reference/directional questions per typical week
               (D30 and 31)

_____ 33. Number of orientation tours

_____ 34. Number of students receiving orientation tours

_____ 35. Contact hours of librarian in-class lectures

_____ 36. Number of students receiving librarian in-class lectures

_____ 37. Contact hours of librarian in-library lectures

_____ 38. Number of students receiving librarian in-library lectures

_____ 39. Number of classes using prepared Bibliographic Instruction
               audio/visual lectures

_____ 40. Number of students receiving Bibliographic Instruction by audio/visual lectures

_____ 41. Total number of Bibliographic Instruction sessions (D33,35, 37, and 39)

_____ 42. Total number of students receiving Bibliographic Instruction (D 34, 36, 38 and 40).

_____ 43. Number of computer-based bibliographic searches provided by librarians

Media Equipment Services
_____ 44. Total number of equipment set-ups

45. Number of equipment set-ups for

    a. Biology Department   _____

    b. Chemistry Department   _____

    c. Communications Department   _____

    d. Dexter Hanley College   _____

    e. Education Department   _____

    f. English Department   _____

    g. Fine Arts Department   _____

    h. Foreign Languages Department _____

    i. History/Political Science Department _____

    j. Human Resources Department   _____

    k. Mathematics/Computer Science Department _____

    l. Military Science Department   _____

    m. Nursing Department   _____

    n. Philosophy Department   _____

    o. Physical Education Department _____

    p. Physical Therapy Department   _____

    q. Physics Department   _____

    r. Psychology Department   _____

    s. School of Management   _____

    t. Sociology/Criminal Justice/ Gerontology Department   _____

    u. Theology/Religious Studies Department _____

App 8

v. Users in the Media Center _____

w. Other _____

_____ 46. Total number of equipment loans (excluding set-ups)

_____ 47. Number of requests filled for media production

_____ 48. Number of media items produced for filled production requests

49. Number of filled production requests and items produced for

a. Slides _____ _____

b. Transparencies _____ _____

c. Classroom videotaping _____ _____

d. Off-air taping _____ _____

e. Non-classroom videotaping _____ _____

f. Video and audio duplicating _____ _____

_____ 50. Number of equipment repairs (in-house and out-of-house) handled

E. HOURS OF SERVICE

_____ 1. Hours per week library public services are available (excluding extended hours)

_____ 2. Hours per week library public services are available (during extended hours)

_____ 3. Hours per week media center services are available

F. FUNDING

_____ 1. Expenditures for books, serials, standing orders, and information services

_____ 2. Average cost per title for books, serials, standing orders, and information services

3. Expenditures for books, serials, standing orders, and information services and average cost per title for

a. Biology Department _____ _____

b. Chemistry Department _____ _____

c. Communications Department _____ _____

d. Dexter Hanley College _____ _____

e. Education Department _____ _____

f. English Department _____ _____

App 9

g. Fine Arts Department _____ _____

h. Foreign Languages Department _____ _____

i. General Funds _____ _____

j. History/Political Science Department _____ _____

k. Human Resources Department _____ _____

l. Mathematics/Computer Science Department _____ _____

m. Military Science Department _____ _____

n. Nursing Department _____ _____

o. Philosophy Department _____ _____

p. Physical Education Department _____ _____

q. Physical Therapy Department _____ _____

r. Physics Department _____ _____

s. Psychology Department _____ _____

t. School of Management _____ _____

u. Sociology/Criminal Justice/ Gerontology Department _____ _____

v. Theology/Religious Studies Department _____ _____

_____ 4. Expenditures for periodicals

_____ 5. Average cost per title for periodicals

6. Expenditures for periodicals and average cost per title for

a. Biology Department _____ _____

b. Chemistry Department _____ _____

c. Communications Department _____ _____

d. Dexter Hanley College _____ _____

e. Education Department _____ _____

f. English Department _____ _____

g. Fine Arts Department _____ _____

h. Foreign Languages Department _____ _____

i. General Funds _____ _____

38

    j. History/Political Science
        Department   _____ _____

    k. Human Resources Department   _____ _____

    l. Mathematics/Computer Science
        Department   _____ _____

    m. Military Science Department   _____ _____

    n. Nursing Department   _____ _____

    o. Philosophy Department   _____ _____

    p. Physical Education Department   _____ _____

    q. Physical Therapy Department   _____ _____

    r. Physics Department   _____ _____

    s. Psychology Department   _____ _____

    t. School of Management   _____ _____

    u. Sociology/Criminal Justice/
        Gerontology Department   _____ _____

    v. Theology/Religious Studies
        Department   _____ _____

7. Expenditures for microforms

8. Total expenditures for print and print media information
    materials (F1, 4 and 7)

9. Expenditures for non-print media

10. Expenditures for print and non-print information
     materials (F8 and 9)

11. Expenditures for binding

12. Expenditures for conservation

13. Expenditures for database fees

14. Expenditures for interlibrary loan changes

15. Expenditures for fees paid to cooperative organizations

16. Other information/access expenditures

17. Total of expenditures for acquisition of information
     materials, enhancement of information materials, and access
     to information materials (F10, 11, 12, 13, 14, 15 and 16)

18. Expenditures for equipment

19. Expenditures for administrative services.

39

_____ 20. Expenditures for salaries and wages of library and media staff (excluding student assistants)

_____ 21. Expenditure for fringe benefits

_____ 22. Expenditures for wages of student assistants

_____ 23. Total expenditures for staff salaries, wages, and fringe benefits (F20, 21, and 22)

_____ 24. Expenditures of federal funds (list each grant following)

_____ 25. Expenditures of other funds (list each grant following)

_____ 26. Grand total of expenditures from the library and media budget (F17, 18, 19, 23, 24, and 25)

_____ 27. University Educational and General Budget, including mandatory transfers

_____ 28. Library and media budget expressed as percentage of the University Educational and General Budget

29. Percentage of the University Educational and General Budget for

   a. the Library alone   _____

   b. the Media Resources Center alone   _____

_____ 30. University Instructional Budget

_____ 31. Library and media budget expressed as percentage of the University Instructional Budget

32. Percentage of the University Instructional Budget for

   a. the Library alone   _____

   b. the Media Resources Center alone   _____

_____ 33. Library and media expenditures expressed per capita FTES (F 26 divided by 19)

G. STAFFING

_____ 1. Number of full-time female administrative and professional staff, head count

_____ 2. Number of part-time female administrative and professional staff, head count

_____ 3. Number of FTE female administrative and professional staff

40

_____ 4. Number of full-time male administrative and professional staff, head count

_____ 5. Number of part-time male administrative and professional staff, head count

_____ 6. Number of FTE male administrative and professional staff

_____ 7. Number of full-time female faculty, head count

_____ 8. Number of part-time female faculty, head count

_____ 9. Number of FTE female faculty

_____ 10. Number of full-time male faculty, head count

_____ 11. Number of part-time male faculty, head count

_____ 12. Number of FTE male faculty

_____ 13. Number of full-time female clerical and technical staff, head count

_____ 14. Number of part-time female clerical and technical staff, head count

_____ 15. Number of FTE female clerical and technical staff

_____ 16. Number of full-time male clerical and technical staff, head count

_____ 17. Number of part-time male clerical and technical staff, head count

_____ 18. Number of FTE male clerical and technical staff

_____ 19. Total number of full-time staff, head count (G1, 4, 7, 10 13, and 16)

_____ 20. Total number of part-time staff, head count (G2, 5, 8, 11, 14, and 17)

_____ 21. Total FTE staff (G3, 6, 9, 12, 15, 18)

_____ 22. Total number of hours of student assistance

23. Number of hours of student assistance for

    a. the Library alone _____

    b. The Media Resources Center alone _____

H. PHYSICAL PLANT

_____ 1. Gross assignable area administered by the library (square feet)

_____ 2. Gross assignable area administered by the media center (square feet)

_____ 3. Gross assignable area administered by the archives (sq.ft.)

_____ 4. Total gross assignable area administered (square feet) (H1, 2, and 3)

_____ 5. Net assignable area administered by the library (square feet)

_____ 6. Net assignable area administered by the media center (square feet)

_____ 7. Net assignable area administered by the archives (square ft.)

_____ 8. Total net assignable area administered (square feet) (H5, 6 and 7)

_____ 9. Seating capacity in the library

_____ 10. Seating capacity in the media center

_____ 11. Seating capacity in the archives

_____ 12. Total seating capacity (H9, 10, and 11)

_____ 13. Library shelf space (linear feet)

_____ 14. Library shelf space (percentage of utilization)

_____ 15. Media Center shelf space (linear feet)

_____ 16. Media Center shelf space (percentage of utilization)

_____ 17. Archives shelf space (linear feet)

_____ 18. Archives shelf space (percentage of utilization)

I. USER POPULATION

_____ 1. Faculty, head count (fall semester)

_____ 2. FTE faculty (fall semester)

_____ 3. Undergraduate students, head count (fall semester)

_____ 4. FTE undergraduate students (fall semester)

_____ 5. Graduate students, head count (fall semester)

UNIVERSITY OF SCRANTON LIBRARY

_____ 6. FTE graduate students (fall semester)

_____ 7. University support staff, head count (fall semester)

_____ 8. Total user community on campus, head count, served by
                the library and Media Center (I1, 3, 5 and 7)

_____ 9. Total FTES population served by the Library and Media
                Center (I4 and 6)

_____ 10. FTES per FTE librarian/professional (I9 divided by
                [G3 plus 6, 9 and 12])

_____ 11. Library exit count

_____ 12. Library Circulation desk registrations (summer session,
                fall, intersession, spring)

            13. Library circulation desk registrations (summer session,
                fall, intersession, spring) for

                a. College of Arts and Sciences   _____

                b. College of Health, Education
                    and Human Resources   _____

                c. School of Management   _____

                d. Hanley College   _____

                e. Graduate School   _____

                f. Faculty   _____

                g. Staff   _____

                h. Alumni   _____

                i. Scranton Prep   _____

                j. NEPIC institutions   _____

                k. Other   _____

            14. Percentage of summer session, fall, intersession,
                spring term enrollees registered at the library
                circulation desk for

                a. College of Arts and Sciences   _____

                b. College of Health, Education &
                    Human Resources   _____

                c. School of Management   _____

                d. Hanley College   _____

                e. Graduate School   _____

43

J. EXTERNAL AFFILIATIONS

    1. Cooperative or contract affiliations (intertype library networks, library public agencies, reference service centers, consortia, etc.)

    2. Special subject collections

    3. Depository collections (government, commercial, etc.)

COVER GRAPHICS

THE NASH LIBRARY
Annual Report

1986-87

GANNON UNIVERSITY
619 Sassafras Street
Erie, Pennsylvania 16541

WEYERHAEUSER LIBRARY
MACALESTER COLLEGE

ANNUAL REPORT

1986/87

ANNUAL REPORT
1986 — 1987

Margaret O. Bruns
1898-1984

**MURRY and LEONIE GUGGENHEIM
MEMORIAL LIBRARY
MONMOUTH COLLEGE
WEST LONG BRANCH, N.J.**

SAGINAW VALLEY STATE COLLEGE
MELVIN J. ZAHNOW LIBRARY
ANNUAL REPORT
1985-86

ɪsity of Wisconsin-Green Bay

ɪ6 annual report

ARNING SOURCES

r for Television Production

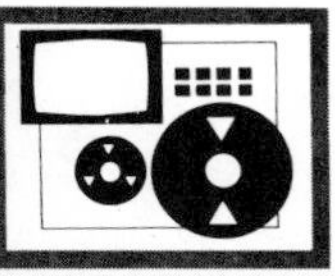

ɪtional Communications

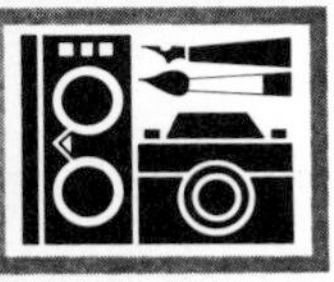

ɪical Support Services

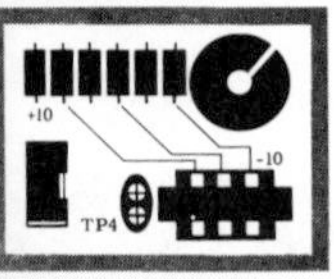

Station WGBW

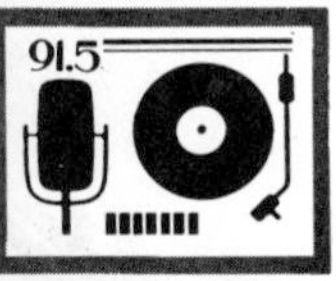

brary Learning Center

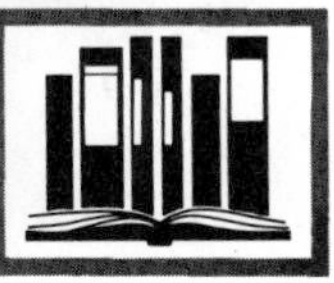

Library/Learning Center

Director's Annual Report
1985/86

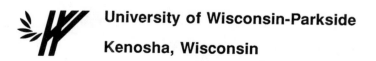 University of Wisconsin-Parkside

Kenosha, Wisconsin

CONTENT GRAPHICS

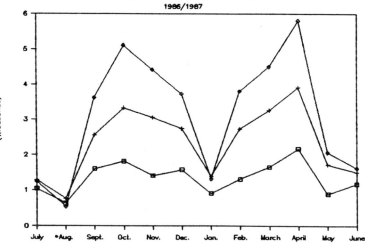

GUGGENHEIM MEMORIAL LIBRARY, MONMOUTH COLLEGE
ATTENDANCE — HOUR
1986/1987

Time	July	Aug	Sept.	Oct.	Nov.	Dec.
8:45 a.m. - 1:00 p.m.	1,037	630	1,604	1,814	1,417	1,580
1:00 p.m. - 5:00 p.m.	1,287	762	2,559	3,354	3,073	2,757
5:00 p.m. - midnight	1,243	541	3,634	5,114	4,432	3,753
Total	3,567	1,933	7,797	10,282	8,922	8,090

Time	Jan.	Feb.	March	April	May	June	Total
8:45 a.m. - 1:00 p.m.	923	1,323	1,666	2,192	899	1,193	16,278
1:00 p.m. - 5:00 p.m.	1,392	2,752	3,293	3,945	1,738	1,518	28,430
5:00 p.m. - midnight	1,330	3,831	4,519	5,804	2,090	1,637	37,928
Total	3,645	7,906	9,478	11,941	4,727	4,348	82,636

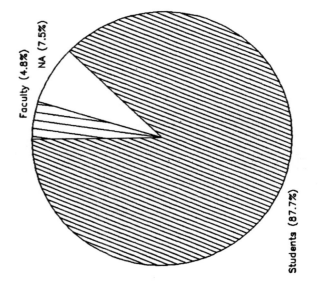

TOTAL CIRCULATION
1986/1987

Faculty (4.8%)

NA (7.5%)

Students (87.7%)

GUGGENHEIM MEMORIAL LIBRARY, MONMOUTH COLLEGE

LIBRARY CIRCULATION

	1985/1986	1986/1987	+ or −
July	1,307	1,081	− 226
August	697	646	− 51
September	1,814	2,624	+ 810
October	3,444	4,043	+ 599
November	3,728	4,732	+ 1,004
December	2,459	2,650	+ 191
January	1,814	1,297	− 517
February	3,709	3,576	− 133
March	3,670	4,454	+ 784
April	5,025	5,019	− 6
May	1,010	1,055	+ 45
June	1,268	1,188	− 80
TOTAL	29,945	32,365	+ 2,420

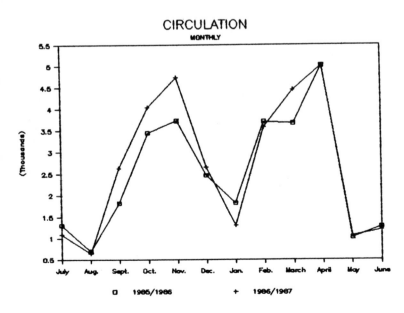

CIRCULATION
MONTHLY

□ 1985/1986   + 1986/1987

57

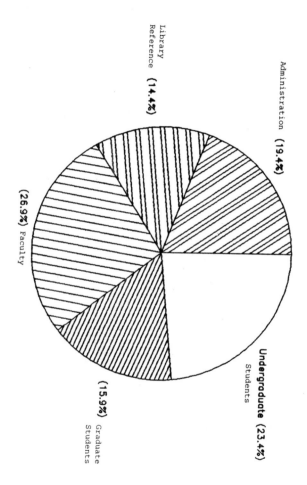

ONLINE SUMMARY

1986/1987

Administration (19.4%)

Library
Reference (14.4%)

(26.9%) Faculty

Undergraduate (23.4%)
Students

(15.9%)
Graduate
Students

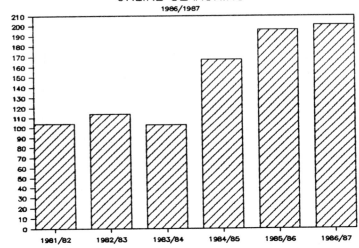

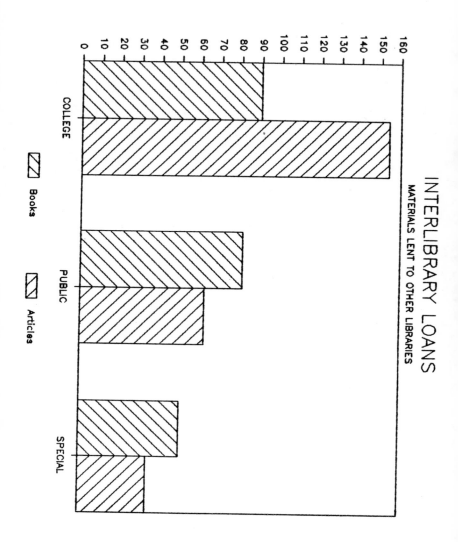

Center for Television Production

[White offset paper]

Educational
Communications

[Blue offset paper]

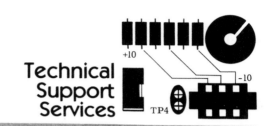

[White offset paper]

Radio
Station
WGBW

91.5

[Blue offset paper]

[White offset paper]

IDA JANE DACUS LIBRARY, WINTHROP COLLEGE

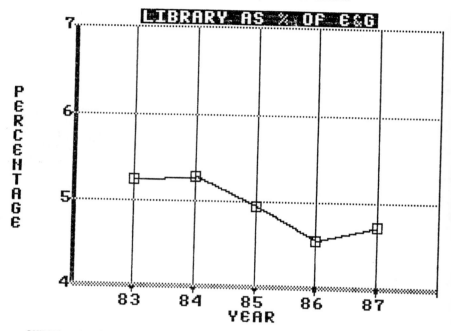

SOURCES: 1983/84-1985/86 are from <u>Winthrop College Financial Report</u> (Unaudited). 1986/87 is based on estimates by the Budget Office and the Dacus Library budget as of January 1, 1987.

IDA JANE DACUS LIBRARY, WINTHROP COLLEGE

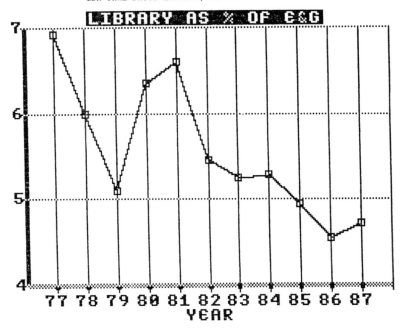

SOURCES: Figures for 1977/78 – 1982/83 are from <u>Winthrop College State Auditor's</u>
<u>Report</u>. 1983/84 – 1985/86 are from unaudited financial reports. 1986/87
is based on estimates by the Budget Office and the Dacus Library budget
as of January 14, 1987.

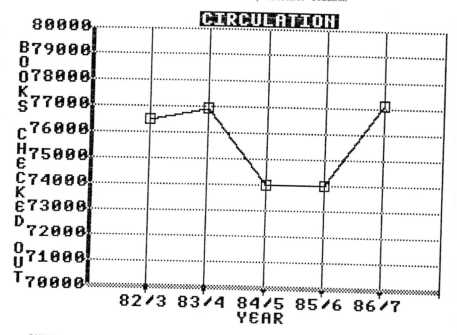

SOURCE: Dacus Library Public Services Statistics

IDA JANE DACUS LIBRARY, WINTHROP COLLEGE

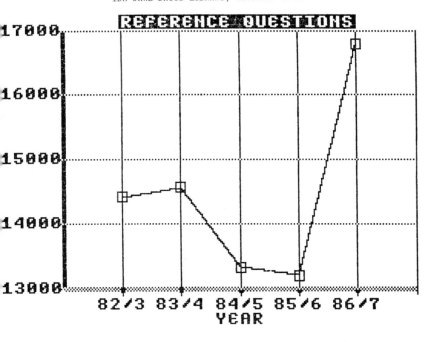

SOURCE: Dacus Library Public Services Statistics.

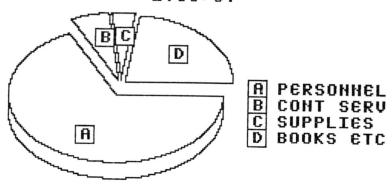

SOURCE: Dacus Library Budget, 1986/87.

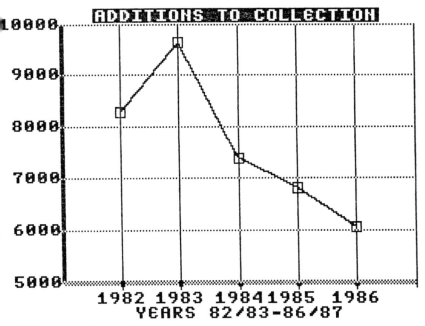

ADDITIONS TO COLLECTION

YEARS 82/83-86/87

SOURCE: Dacus Library Collection Statistics
NOTE: 1983/84 includes a large collection of gift books.

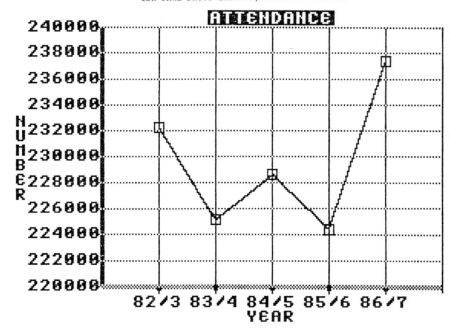

SOURCE: Dacus Library Public Services Statistics.

ANNUAL REPORTS (FULL)

ELLEN CLARKE BERTRAND LIBRARY

Annual Report 1985-86

Bucknell University

Format:

Paper size and weight: 8.5" x 11.0"; 20 lb. bond

Cover size and weight: 8.5" x 11.0"; 65 lb. linen

B/W text; beige cover with "rota" brown type and graphics

Binding: side-stitch

Production:

Editor: Ann de Klerk, Director of Library Services

Logo design: Steve Neuton, Neuton Advertising Agency, Port Treverton, PA

Cover design: in-house

Printed in the University Print Shop; offset

Number of pages: 10 (excluding covers)

Number of copies printed: 550

Stand-alone publication

Distribution:

Sent to University president, chief academic officer, vice presidents, deans, directors of other units on campus, library staff, library advisory committee, faculty, library friends group, consortia libraries

Disseminated by campus mail and U.S.P.S.

ELLEN CLARKE BERTRAND LIBRARY

ANNUAL REPORT

1985-86

BUCKNELL

Director of Library Services, Ann M. de Klerk, M.L.S.

Assistant to the Director of Library Services, Judith Compton-Ellis, M.A.T.

Assistant Director for Automated Services, Laurene E. Lozoski, M.L.S.

Assistant Director for Public Services, JoAnne Young, M.L.S., Ph.D.

Assistant Director for Technical Services, Nancy Barrelle, M.A., M.L.S.

Collection Development and Acquisitions Librarian, George M. Jenks, M.A., M.L.S.

Serials Librarian, Chia-Ching Chang, M.A.L.S.

Head Catalog Librarian, Paul W. Boytinck, M.A., M.L.S.

Catalog Librarian, Zoya E. Jenks, M.S.L.S.

Circulation Supervisor, Marcia Hoffman, B.S.

Head, Reference Department, Nancy S. Weyant, M.S.L.S.

Reference Librarian, Debora Cheney, M.L.S.

Reference Librarian, Sharon A. Malecki, M.L.S.

Reference Librarian, Arlieda Ries, M.L.S.

Reference Librarian, Loanne L. Snavely, M.L.S., M.S.T.

ELLEN CLARKE BERTRAND LIBRARY
ANNUAL REPORT
1985/86

The high point of the year was the celebration of the formal reopening of the Ellen Clarke Bertrand Library, which took place May 3, during Spring Weekend. Although the weather was cold and blustery, it was also bright, like our spirits, and we were honored that Mr. Charles Watts, Trustee and 11th President of Bucknell, was on hand to give the keynote address.

PHYSICAL FACILITIES

The goals of our building program were met: space for users, space for the collections to grow, and space for special facilities including the LaFayette Butler Reading Room for Special Collections/University Archives, the library lab, and the twenty-four hour study.

The use of the library has increased dramatically, in keeping with reported experience. Users' expectations are raised with a new building. Even though the number of reader seats tripled and is now higher than the American Library Association standard for an institution of our size, we were extremely overcrowded at exam time in May. During 1986/87 we will address concerns about security, noise, food and drink. Student involvement in finding solutions is being encouraged.

It was a year of intense activity for the entire library staff: the addition was completed, and we planned and executed the move of the entire collection and many offices for the second time in eight months. The months between December and May were incredibly hectic, as contractors, physical plant personnel, and library staff completed work on the building in readiness for May 3. Job supervisor Calvin Swank (Kline Associates) made a major contribution to the smoothness of the entire construction project through his courteous and expert handling of many problems. Physical plant personnel, directed by Mr. Robert Naugle, were unfailingly cooperative and hard-working. The wise counsel, broad experience in building, and helpful involvement in matters great and small of Vice-

President John Zeller are gratefully acknowledged. He was always responsive to the needs of the library, its staff and its users. Vice-President Wendell Smith's dedication to and support of the long-term goals of the library were a major factor in the successful completion of this endeavor. The library staff remained in good spirits through multiple moves, much noise, disruption, and dust.

SERVICES

I. Public Services

In public services, the end-user searching program was planned and implemented on a pilot basis beginning Spring Semester 1986. At the reference desk we studied the use patterns, and as a result, allocated additional staff during heavy use periods. The availability of the library lab will enhance our library instruction program. The entire reference collection is now housed in one place, in contrast to three locations on two floors; this in itself constitutes improved service to the university community.

Additional staff in the circulation department has allowed regular staff coverage during the evening and on weekends. Periodicals staff and circulation staff brought the periodical collection into good order following the move, making periodicals more readily available to our users. Consolidation of microform equipment in one place, adjacent to a continuously staffed service desk, is an effort to make this non-traditional medium easier to use.

Government documents, an official resource collection for the citizens of Union County, as well as Bucknell, was inspected by the U.S. Government Documents inspector and given high ratings in all categories, including service. Interlibrary loan has increased again -- this year by 35%. Computerized database searching, with the many citations that it generates, created a greater demand for materials not owned by the library.

The first volume in the Ellen Clarke Bertrand Library's Limited Edition Series, The Man Who Loved Islands by D.H. Lawrence, was jointly published by the Press of Appletree Alley and the library. The edition of 150 copies is almost sold out.

Significant additions to the Special Collections include a gift of 19 Golden Cockerel Press imprints from Mr. Thomas Yoseloff and the purchase of several Kelmscott Press books, made possible by the Friends of the Library. Both of these important new additions were featured in exhibits. Other exhibits have included interesting book bindings and Bucknell history. The expanded building includes attractive exhibit space in the lobby and near the LaFayette Butler Reading Room for Special Collections and University Archives. During the coming year we hope to mount a number of distinctive exhibits relating to authors, books, printing, and, also to the University.

II. Technical Services

There were two major events in technical services. First was the combining of the ordering procedures and record maintenance for serials and periodicals within technical services. Out of 2,400 periodical titles, 1,900 are now ordered via Faxon, a subscription agent, thus reducing the clerical procedures required when individual orders are sent directly to publishers. The periodicals staff is in the process of reviewing all records and correcting information about periodicals, a long-term project. The second event was the completion of the conversion of card catalog records for all books by the catalog department.

AUTOMATION AND ONLINE CATALOG

All 300,000 book records are now in machine readable form in preparation for the implementation of an online catalog as part of a total automated system. We learned at the May Board of Trustees meeting that the integrated automated library system for Bucknell had been funded. The Task Force on Automated Library Systems developed a detailed planning strategy for the entire project early this year. We are planning to purchase a system during 1987, and have it operational no later than September, 1988. The installation of an integrated library system will keep Bucknell state-of-the-art in regard to access to information. It also places us in a position to take full advantage of future developments in information technology.

STAFF DEVELOPMENT

A performance appraisal seminar was held in Fall 1985, attended by most of the professional staff and a significant number of support staff. The support staff evaluation policy and forms are now completed, and will be utilized during 86/87. Performance measures will be developed during the coming year.

Two librarians attended the 1986 Institute on Library Analytical Skills sponsored by the Association of Research Libraries, Office of Management Studies, and two librarians went to a Library Orientation Instruction Exchange conference on computerized and end-user database searching. Other staff development and continuing education activities include database training, microcomputer workshops, and a writing workshop.

Additional staff is required in order to continue to provide current services, and to introduce needed new ones. Professional staff size has remained constant over the past decade.

PLANNING AND PRIORITIES

Our annual planning day was held in January this year, to coordinate with the budget cycle. Media Services is now part of the library organization, reporting to the Assistant Director for Public Services. We are pleased that another resource is now integrated into the wide range of information resources offered by the library. A return to the Chiefs/Assistant Directors organizational pattern has been effective, and we continue to explore ways to improve communication and to modify our organizational structure.

During the coming year we shall develop the requirements for and select an integrated library system. We continue to have as goals the integration of library instruction into the University's academic program, and the revitalization of our Friends of the Library program.

CONCLUSION

Now that the long-awaited building expansion and renovation is complete, we look forward to the online catalog. As importantly, we look forward to having the time and opportunity to expand our whole range of services to the University community.

Ann de Klerk
Director of Library Services
November, 1986

Services to Students and Faculty

Circulating Books loaned:	1984/85	1985/86
dents	32,595	32,418
lty	8,407	8,251
er	22,061	21,669
Sub-total	(63,063)	(62,338)
erve books.	42,044	44,084
ia (tapes, headsets, calculators)	125	41
. Theses, L'Agendas, Local History.	269	344
TOTAL	105,501	106,807

Periodicals loaned:		
dents	2,557	1,336
ulty	3,190	2,753
er	797	498
TOTAL	6,544	4,587

| norecords loaned. . . . . | 775 | 776 |

| GRAND TOTAL . . . . | 112,045 | 111,535 |

Interlibrary Loan

Service to Bucknell Users

k requests (including fiche, docs., etc.)	570	919
riodical requests.	1,527	2,366
TOTAL	2,097	3,285

Service to Other Libraries

ok requests	2,170	2,641
riodical requests.	1,519	1,885
TOTAL	3,689	4,526

| GRAND TOTAL . . . . | 5,786 | 7,81] |

Acquisitions

sh requests received	531	40
sh requests returned as duplicates	141	7
sh requests ordered	384	31
tal requests received.	8,366	8,22
tal requests returned as duplicates.	2,983	3,04
tal requests ordered	4,860	4,67

	1984/85	1_
Total volumes, books and periodicals, beginning of fiscal year	443,761	4
Added by purchase	13,799	
Added by gifts and exchange.	470	
Added by bound periodicals	3,472	
Withdrawn books and periodicals.	8,547	
TOTAL VOLUMES, end of fiscal year.	452,955	4
Titles added	13,286	
Titles withdrawn	4,479	
*Net titles added	8,807	
Titles, end of fiscal year	294,522	3
Periodical titles currently received	2,341	
Other periodical titles.	1,762	
Total periodical titles, end of fiscal year. . . .	4,103	
**Periodical volumes, end of fiscal year	65,100	
Phonorecords, titles, end of fiscal year	1,522	
discs, end of fiscal year.	2,673	
Cassettes, end of fiscal year.	243	
Pamphlets, end of fiscal year.	16,675	
Government Publications added.	25,658	
Government Publications withdrawn.	16,618	
Government Publications, end of fiscal year. . . .	239,344	2
Government Publications in microfiche (included above)	111,555	1
Maps, end of fiscal year	3,495	
Microfilm, reels, end of fiscal year	11,799	
Microprint, cards, end of fiscal year.	27,950	
Microfiche, sheets, end of fiscal year	186,746	2

---

  * Does not include sound recordings, maps,
      microforms, periodicals or multimedia
 ** Included in total volumes

Expenditures for materials

Single orders	$129,433	11
Standing orders (books).	78,344	8
Approval books	141,508	15
Periodicals.	262,190	32
TOTAL	$611,475	68

Staff Changes - July 1, 1985 - June 30, 1986

Appointments:

Karen Dudziak	Reference	August 26, 1985
Nancy Barrelle	Technical Services	September 1, 1985
Thomas Diehl	Shipping/Receiving	September 9, 1985
Arlieda Ries	Reference	October 14, 1985
JoAnne Young	Public Services	November 1, 1985
Ann Gibson	Reference	March 25, 1986
Cindy Whitmoyer	Circulation	May 5, 1986
Marcia Hoffman	Circulation	June 2, 1986

Resignations:

Joel Clemmer	Facilities Planning	July 17, 1985
Patricia Peroni	Reference	July 31, 1985
Anne Rowland	Cataloging	July 31, 1985
Karen Dudziak	Reference	December 21, 1985
Ann Schreck	Reference	February 28, 1986
Sandra Inch	Circulation	April 14, 1986
Virginia Weidenhamer	Acquisitions	May 31, 1986
Barbara Selsam	Reference	June 20, 1986
Alice Dowling	Circulation	June 30, 1986

On Leave:

Nancy Weyant	Reference	Fall 1985

Transfers:

Jean Bingaman	Circulation to Reference June 21, 1986

ORGANIZATIONS, CONFERENCES, MEETINGS, WORKSHOPS AND COMMITTEES IN WHICH BUCKNELL LIBRARIANS PARTICIPATED:

American Library Association

Annual Conference
Midwinter Meeting
Government Documents Roundtable (GODORT)
Library Information and Technology Association
Intellectual Freedom Committee
Resources and Technical Services Division

American Society for Information Science

Annual Conference
Mid-year Conference
Special Interest Group on Library Automation and Networks

Pennsylvania Library Association

College and Research Libraries Division
Annual Conference
Executive Committee
Publications and Research Materials Committee
Library Instruction Committee
Long Range Planning Committee
PLA/GODART Spring Conference
Microcomputer Meeting on Optical Discs
On-line Services Roundtable
Technical Services Roundtable
Poster Fair, exhibit of Bertrand Library publications

PALINET

Cataloging Workshop
Crosstalk XVI Training Session and Workshop
OCLC for Public Services Librarian Workshop
Reference Use of OCLC Workshop

Association of College and Research Libraries

National Conference
Delaware Valley Chapter Board
Special Libraries Association
Bibliographic Instruction Section
Communications Committee
Advisory Council
Executive Committee

OTHERS

Association of Research Libraries, Office of Management Studies
Library Analytical Skills Institute
Ben Franklin Seminars on Microcomputer Use
Keeping an Electronic Bibliography Seminar
Reaching for Information: Micro communications/databases
Statistical Packages for Microcomputing
Beta Phi Mu
Central PA Consortium/Women's Studies Program
LOEX Library Instruction Conference "Bibliographic Instruction
and Computer Database Searching"
Middle States Association, Evaluation Team Library Association
National Women Studies Association
New Technologies for Resources Sharing Workshop
North American Serials Interest Group
Pennsylvania Citizens for Better Libraries

SERVICE TO BUCKNELL

Arts and Sciences Curriculum Committee
Association For the Arts Committee
Bucknell Dialog Program
Complimentary Activities Committee
Engineering Curriculum Committee
Freshman Residential College Committee
Graduate Studies Committee
Honorary Degrees Committee

PUBLICATIONS AND PAPERS PRESENTED

Boytinck, Paul. Review of FLAME INTO BEING; THE LIFE AND WORK OF
D.H. LAWRENCE by Anthony Burgess. London: Hedinemann, 1985.
For Spring issue of Queen's Quarterly.

Boytinck, Paul. Review of MAX BEERBOHM, OR, THE DANDY DANTE; REREADI
WITH MIRRORS by Robert Viscusi. Baltimore; London: Johns Hopkins
University Press, 1986. For Summer Issue of Queen's Quarterly.

Cheney, Debora. Database Review CIS Index. Congressional Informatio
Services. Vendor: Dialog, File no. 101. Appeared in Government
Publications Review 12 (1985). 662-64.

Cheney, Debora. Book review on Subject Guide to U.S. Government
Reference Sources. Appeared in Government Publications Review
13 (1986): 287-88, 1986.

de Klerk, Ann. PLA Buildings and Equipment Roundtable Preconference.
"Library Building Planning." October, 1985

Jenks, George. "Recent Articles and Dissertations," RAILROAD
HISTORY 152 (Spring 1985); 146-48 and 153 (Autumn 1986): 123.

Malecki, Sharon and Cheney, Debora. "Industrial Directories:
A Closer Look" submitted to RG May 6, 1986.

Snavely, Loanne, editor, BIS Newsletter. The Newsletter of the
ALA/ACRL Bibliographic Instruction Section. Fall 1985, Vol. 2,
No. 2; Spring 1986, Vol. 3, No. 1.

Young, JoAnne. "Libraries Organizing to Lobby." Presentation
at Pennsylvania Council of Library Networks and Pennsylvania Library
Association, Northeast Chapter.

REINERT/ALUMNI MEMORIAL LIBRARY

Annual Report 1986-1987

Creighton University

Format:

Paper size and weight: 8.5" x 11.0"; 20 lb. bond

Cover size and weight: 8.5" x 11.0"; 65 lb. Cover stock

B/W text; clay color cover with black type and graphics

Binding: plastic spiral

Production:

Editor: Raymond B. Means, Library Director

Graphics designer: Mike Poma, Reference staff

Printed in the University Print Shop; offset

Number of pages: 22 (excluding covers)

Number of copies: 30

Stand-alone publication

Distribution:

Sent to University president, chief academic officer, vice presidents, deans, librarians, library advisory committee, consortia libraries, selection of other libraries

Disseminated by campus mail and U.S.P.S.

ANNUAL REPORT

1986 - 1987

Reinert/Alumni Memorial Library

Creighton University

Omaha, Nebraska

DIRECTOR'S LOOK AT 1986-87

The previous twelve month period is the first time in six ye‍
that the Library has not been under some type of physical constructi‍
It presented the staff with a time for intellectual growth and preparat‍
for the future of the Library. This past year was a time when the sta‍
reflected on libraries as not just walls and stacks and circulat‍
books but rather that libraries are about learning, the acquiring ‍
sharing of knowledge.

HIGHLIGHTS

Three staff members presented papers at professional meetings

    Staff leadership was expended on behalf of the profession in t‍
Metro area and the state

A plan of operation for library automation was written

    Classroom teaching by the Library staff as a credit course w‍
inaugurated

The Circulation Department underwent an organizational study

    A new departmental budget reporting form went into use

Periodical titles were cut and no new titles were added following
cost analysis

    A new faculty check out policy was adopted in consultation wi‍
the Library Committee

A staff self study, "Incentatives in the Workplace", was conducted.

Two employees resigned during 1986-87 and have been replaced, o‍
by a new employee and one by internal University transfer. The sta‍
of the Reinert/Alumni Memorial Library is dedicated to giving excelle‍
library service and is worthy of this public statement of satisfacti‍
on the part of the Director.

Equally dedicated was the Library Committee for 1986-87. The membe‍

f the Committee were Father Thomas Hoffman, chairperson, Dr.'s Gary
Dean, Don Yoder, Eleftheria Bernidaki-Aldous, and student Paul Schaub.
The Committee approved a new checkout policy for faculty and vetoed
a cost plus policy for computer searches requested by non-university
patrons.

As Director I wish to thank all those who contributed to the success
of the library in 1986-1987. Thank you.

THE YEAR IN REVIEW 1986 - 87

Highlights from the four departments which make up the Reinert/Alu
Memorial Library

Amnesty Day resulted in the return of books with a value of $636.0

Some cuts in journal titles were made; the problem of infla
periodical prices loomed larger than ever.

The Government Publications collection received an overall rat
of Excellent from the Government inspector.

Developed a one credit hour course on library skills offered
the fall semester.

Purchased 6,492 new monographs, 2.5% less than last year. B
prices rose 5.9% over the previous year.

Received two grants for retrospective conversion of the collect
onto computer readable form. (1) $2,500.00 from LSCA Title II
(2) $1,500.00 from the Eastern Library System.

4% of the books added to the collection this year were gif
Nonprint materials made up 11% of the new items added.

The Media Department was merged with the Circulation Department.

The Standing Order file and the Periodical holdings list are
available by computer printout.

Developed a term paper clinic for students and a hands on compu
search workshop for faculty.

Increased automation activity in Technical Services with on l
ordering from our primary vendor and a new software package
cataloging

NUMBERS OF INTEREST 1986 - 87

Added to the shelves: 9,691 bound volumes

9,989 microfiche

3,103 government publications

Loaned 1,134 books and 404 photocopies to other libraries - 15% incr
over 1985-86.

Borrowed 563 books and 569 photocopies from other libraries - 42% increase over 1985-86.

Answered 11,267 reference questions.

Toured for orientation 1,107 students.

Turnstyle count 442,938; checked out 83,477 items from the Circulation desk.

Marketing and Management department from the College of Business Administration was the largest academic department user of computer searches.

Net cost of computer searches was $3,232.90 of which the Library paid $77.81. The remainder was paid by the users. Graduate students accounted for 35% of the computer searches.

Averaging all disciplines, the cost of an academic book is $33.66.

Filed 44,203 cards in the card catalog; that is 36 feet 10 inches.

Withdrew 738 books from the collection.

LIBRARY STAFF 1986 - 87

DEPARTMENT   NAME & POSITION

Administration   Means, Director (10)
                               Swanek, Assistant to the Director (21)
                               Browning, Secretary (9)
                               Garrett, Evening Supervisor (4)

Circulation & Media   Chase, Department Chair (17)
                               McPherson, Media Coordinator (3)
                               D'Agosta, Curriculum Lab. (1)

Reference   Nash, Department Chair (6)
                               LeBeau, DIALOG (4)
                               Poma, Outreach (4)
                               Warzyn, Government Publications (4)
                               VanWaart, Interlibrary Loan (1)

Serials   Swanek, Department Chair (21)
                               Clark, Clerk (2)

Technical Services   Grabe, Department Chair (15)
                               Payne, Cataloger (12)
                               Evans, Acquisitions (12)
                               Golden, Processing (13)
                               Hilton, Cataloging (7)
                               O'Neill, Acquisitions (8)

() Number of years at Creighton

                          ORGANIZATION
                    V.P. For Academic Affairs
                               !
                               !
                        Library Director
                               !
                               !Administrative Assistant
                               !
              Evening Supervisor !Secretary
                               !
!!!
        !   !   !   !
        !   !   !   !
   Serials   Reference   Technical Services   Circulation
     Period   Inst.   Acquisition   Media
     S.O.   Gov. Pub.   Cataloging   Curr.Lab
     Binding   Comp. Search

The staff of the Reinert/Alumni Library has seven members with M.L.S. degrees. The total staff has 153 years of service at Creighton. During this past year, exclusive of the Director, the staff used 520 hours of time for off campus education and service events. These hours represent a major committment by the University to the professional education and training of the Library staff, both professional and non professional.

STAFF MEMBERSHIPS :

The staff is represented by membership at these professional organizations:

American Library Association
   Divisions, Sections, and Round tables
Nebraska Library Association
Metropolitan Area Librarians Club
International Council of Library Association Executives
Paraprofessional Organization of N.L.A.
Delta Phi Mu
Catholic Library Association

STAFF CONTRIBUTIONS :

Official contributions to the profession include:

American Library Association, Membership Task Force
International Council of Library Association Executives, Officer, Board of Directors
Nebraska Library Association, Officer, Board of Directors
Nebraska Library Association, Section Chairperson
Nebraska Library Association, Committees
Eastern Library System, Committees
Omaha Metropolitan Area Librarians Club, Chairperson
Nebraska Online User's Group, Coordinator
Metro Omaha National Library Week, Committee

LeBeau, "Librarians and the Law: Is It Time For Malpractice Insurance?" (paper)

Poma, "Library Instruction for the Educationally Disadvantaged" (paper)

Nash, "Networking in Nebraska: Yours, Mine or Ours" (moderator)

  "Reciprocal Borrowing in Nebraska" (document)

  "Membership Directory for NLA, C&U" (pamphlet)

Grabe, "Proposed Automated Library System Requirements" (document)

UNIVERSITY BUDGET

Account	July 1, 1986	Revised March 87	Expended	Balance
Salaries	386,950.00	386,950.00	376,770.68	10,179.32
Operating Exp.	36,780.00	36,780.00	36,385.95	394.05
Archives	4,114.00	4,114.00	2,001.21	2,112.79
Preservation	18,000.00	18,000.00	18,009.28	- 9.28
Serials	200,700.00	216,542.79*	216,051.73	491.06
Books	207,931.00	192,088.21*	189,661.01	2,427.20

*March, 1987, $15,842.79 was transfered from Books - General to pay overages in the Serials account.

BALANCE $15,595.14

RESTRICTED ACCOUNTS

Name	Balance July 1, 1986	Deposits	Disbursements	Balance June 30, 1987
Miscellaneous	4,280.57	3,685.75	4,764.46	3,201.86
Photocopy	2,501.55	7,797.61	8,794.56	1,504.60
History 009	2,968.49	0.0	0.0	2,968.49
History 032	667.66	0.0	0.0	667.66
Millard	7,044.07	4,996.79	4,655.36	7,385.50
Fines and Forfeitures	2,052.02	13,469.26	12,934.86	2,586.42
DIALOG	284.23	3,167.43	2,595.24	856.42

GRANTS

	Grant	Expended	Balance
Eastern Library System	1,500.00	1,500.00	0.0
Nebraska Library Commission	2,500.00	2,500.00	0.0

Total expended by the Reinert/Alumni Library 1986-1987 = $879,624.34

EXPENDITURES PER DEPARTMENT
JULY 1, 1986 - JUNE 30, 1987

Department	Materials	Standing Orders	Periodicals	Total
Accounting	1,850.00	5,500.00	1,560.00	8,910.00
American Studies	1,450.00	120.00		1,570.00
Atmospheric Science	1,400.00	500.00	1,567.00	3,517.00
Biology	11,300.00	8,000.00	15,731.00	35,031.00
Chemistry	5,500.00	9,500.00	19,035.00	33,440.00
Classics	4,800.00	250.00	2,460.00	7,510.00
Computer Science	3,500.00			3,500.00
Economics	4,000.00	4,500.00	4,678.00	12,678.00
Education	9,800.00	975.00	3,511.00	14,286.00
English & Speech	17,700.00	4,000.0000	3,776.00	25,476.00
Fine Arts	6,500.00	275.00	514.00	7,289.00
History	16,800.00	4,500.00	3,951.00	24,891.00
International Relations	3,800.00	300.00		4,100.00
Journalism	3,800.00	500.00	448.00	4,748.00
Management/ Marketing	6,000.00	6,000.00	4,984.00	17,252.00
Math	10,691.00	3,200.00	15,860.00	29,751.00
Modern Language	4,800.00	750.00		5,500.00
Philosophy	9,200.00	725.00	2,355.00	12,280.00
Physical Education	3,000.00	125.00	916.00	4,041.00
Physics	9,800.00	2,700.00	26,078.00	38,578.00
Political Science	6,400.00	1,750.00	1,982.00	10,132.00
Psychology	10,900.00	875.00	7,917.00	19,692.00
Sociology	9,000.00	500.00	2,520.000	12,109.00
Theology	14,475.00	2,650.00	2,984.00	20,109.00
General & Reference	31,465.00	19,800.00	4,599.00	55,864.00

HOLDINGS BY CLASS

JULY 1, 1987

Library of Congress No.	Department	7-1-86	W/D	Added	7-1-87
A	General	2,272	53	61	2,280
B-BJ	Philosophy	7,865	21	223	8,067
BF	Psychology	6,058	19	161	6,200
BL-BX	Theology	25,001	127	1,015	25,889
C-F	History	41,648	91	1,002	42,559
G-GT	Anthropology	3,027	10	92	3,109
GV	P.E. & Dance	1,674	9	72	1,737
H-HA	Statistics	1,355	8	70	1,417
HB-HE	Economics	21,685	20	466	22,131
HF-HJ	Management & Marketing	9,186	33	361	9,514
HM-HX	Sociology	11,790	36	527	12,281
J	Political Sci.	8,361	11	271	8,621
K	Law	3,550	35	223	3,738
L	Education	14,723	28	437	15,132
M	Music	1,948	7	45	1,986
N	Art	5,210	3	160	5,367
P-PN	Language	18,832	36	391	19,187
PQ	Romance Lit.	6,764	2	86	6,848
PR	English Lit.	21,472	17	453	21,908
PS	American Lit.	10,229	26	226	10,429
PT	Germanic Lit	3,211	1	59	3,269
PZ	Childrens Lit	1,353	4	41	1,390
Q	General Sci.	1,940	18	91	2,013
QA	Math	10,065	13	381	10,433
QB-QC	Physics	7,767	3	280	8,044
QD	Chemistry	4,078	3	94	4,169
QE-QZ	Biology	10,162	7	347	10,502

Library of Congress No.	Department	7-1-86	W/D	Added	7-1-8
R	Medicine	4,168	27	317	4,458
S	Agriculture	788	1	31	818
T-V	Technology	6,849	14	277	7,112
Z1-1000	Library Science	2,185	8	85	2,262
Z1001-	Bibliography	2,150	45	81	2,186

TOTAL COLLECTION
AS OF JUNE 30, 1987

I. Books

    Bound

General Collection	270,775	
Reference	9,151	
Rare Books	1,384	
TOTAL BOUND		281,310

    Micro

Film	867	
Fiche	19,278	
Ultra Fiche	18,902	
TOTAL MICRO		39,029

TOTAL BOOKS   **320,339**

II. Periodicals

Current subscriptions	1,539
Bound volumes	40,508
Current newspapers	33

III. Non-Print Pieces   (not including periodical & Government Publication holdings)

Microfilm	11,434
Microfiche	96,526
Ultrafiche	19,089
Audio Cassettes	1,696
Phonodiscs	1,481
Video Cassettes	680
Filmstrips	150
Motion Pictures	41
Kits	6
Slides	4,451
Computer Software	31
Transparencies	24

IV. Government Publications
    Paper   39,317
    Microfilm   769
    Microfiche/Ultrafiche   28,411

V. Summary of Total Library Holdings
    Bound Volumes   361,135
    Micro Film Reels   15,851
    Micro Fiche Pieces   651,767

CATALOGING STATISTICS

JULY 1, 1986 - JUNE 30, 1987

	Titles	Volumes
New books cataloged*	6,857	7,082
Nonprint/media cataloged	125	909
Government publications cataloged	97	101
New serials cataloged	75	299
TOTAL CATALOGED	7,154	8,391
Books processed:		
Stacks	6,716	7,418
Reference	222	934
Rare Books	12	17
Theses	3	3
Juvenile Books	60	60
TOTAL BOOKS PROCESSED	7,013	8,432
Books cataloged and processed for Jesuit Community Library	70	73
Nonprint/media processed:		
Audiocassettes	23	62
Videocassettes	65	73
Filmstrips	9	23
Motion Pictures	2	2
Microfiche (non-periodical)	6	557
Microfilm	0	6
Kits	0	0
Maps	3	3
Slides	2	153
Portfolios	1	1
Phonodiscs	2	11
Computer Software	12	18
TOTAL NONPRINT/MEDIA PROCESSED	125	909
Gifts**	0	365
Recataloged	1,842	2,188
Retrospective Conversion (THL LSCA Grant)	1,951	2,308
Books withdrawn:		
Stacks	371	491
Reference	50	247
TOTAL WITHDRAWN	421	738

*Includes 365 gift books
**Included in books processed

	Cards	Feet	Inches
Cards filed in the public catalog:			
Author-Title	24,802	20'8"	248.0
Subject	19,401	16'2"	194.0
TOTAL CARDS FILED:	44,203	36'10"	442.0

Original cataloging   213 titles (2.9%)

OCLC "Hit" Rate: 97%

Duplicates located &
  returned: 73
  At a savings of: $1,997.24

Books mended: 4,054
                43 (Record album jackets)

Average purchase price of
  academic book: $33.66***

***Source: 1987 BOWKER ANNUAL OF LIBRARY & BOOK TRADE INFORMATION.

NEW MATERIALS	VOLUMES
Books purchased:	7,082
Gifts	365
Nonprint	908
TOTAL:	8,356

Print
(Purchased)
85%

Gifts 4%

Nonprint/
Media 11%

CIRCULATION STATISTICS

FACULTY	YEAR 1986/87
Books	6,431
Periodicals	596
Government Publications	146
Reference	145
TOTAL	**7,318**

STUDENTS	
Books	39,342
Government Publications	390
Graduate Semester Loan	3,372
Reserves	26,261
TOTAL	**69,365**

MISCELLANEOUS	
Browsing	588
Curriculum Laboratory	784
Pamphlets	583
Annual Reports	234
Cliff Notes	255
Media	4,350
TOTAL	**6,794**

GRAND TOTAL	**83,477**

ANNUAL TURNSTYLE COUNT

MONTH	YEAR 1986/87
July	14,643
August	14,684
September	42,607
October	61,606
November	53,312
December	30,324
January	22,990
February	60,376
March	49,841
April	60,435
May	19,291
June	12,829
TOTAL	442,938

STATISTICS REFERENCE
1986/1987

	Volumes
Reference Stacks	8,566
Ready Reference*	508
Atlas Case	77
TOTAL General Reference	9,151
TOTAL Storage	2,708
TOTAL Indexes and Abstracts (70 titles)	4,868
TOTAL Microfiche (27 titles)	23,356

QUESTIONS	REFERENCE TOTAL	AVERAGE PER DAY
Information	4,024	12.3
Reference	7,243	22.1
TOTAL	11,267	34.4
Telephone	1,895	5.8
Government Documents	605	1.8

TOTAL SERVICE DAYS   328.5

USAGE BY GROUPS

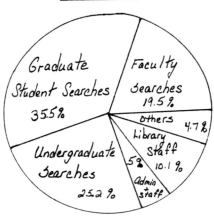

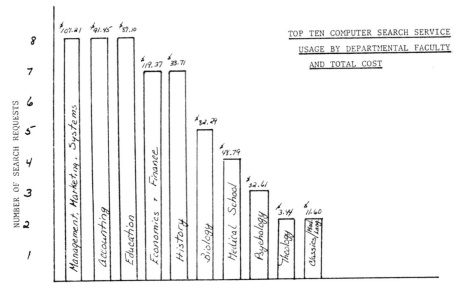

TOP TEN COMPUTER SEARCH SERVICE
USAGE BY DEPARTMENTAL FACULTY
AND TOTAL COST

DEPARTMENTS

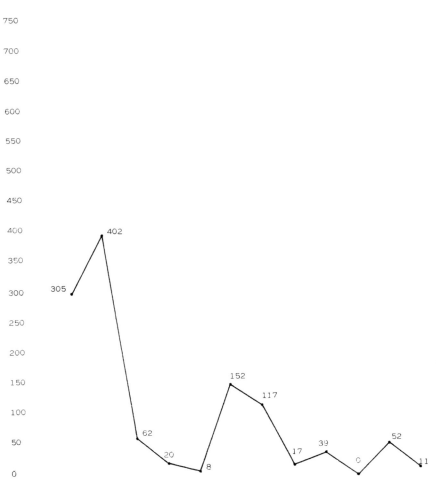

AUG SEPT OCT NOV DEC JAN FEB MARCH APRIL MAY JUNE JULY

LIBRARY INSTRUCTION
PRIMARY POPULATION REACHED = 1107
OTHERS REACHED = 78
GRAND TOTAL = 1185

800

750

700

650

600

550

500

450

400   402

350

300   305

250

200

150   152
              117
100

50   62   17   39   52
         20   11
            8   0

0

	ITEMS RECEIVED			ITEMS WITHDRAWN							Notes
	paper cards	fiche cards	newly cat.	paper cards	fiche cards	cat.	to REF	to LEN	to TECH	WITH paper/fiche cards	
Jul	273	393	10	414	13	2	10	2	62	35	weeded ED and EP
Aug	282	704	11	103	184	4	18	5	84	148	
Sep	286	440	6	663	9	1	24	2	81	50	W/D Energy Rsch Abst (dropped) & 'no index' Gov't Rpts Annot
Oct	229	776	11	195	1130	7	36	1	77	34	
Nov	205	343	3	148	4	--	15	2	55	27	
Dec	267	489	6	614	239	--	17p 196m	1	49	73	W/D incl. tallied items from W/D list 86-3
Jan	258	231	17	249	40	9	11	1	4	165	W/D mostly Census prelim. data superseded
Feb	243	326	11	1168	228	3	12	2	53	18	W/D incl. old area wage surveys, cities
Mar	282	585	2	1028	6	53	12	1	84	38	
Apr	235	482	5	16	175	--	39	2	79	148	1 General collection
May	248	104	4	185	3	--	14	1	67	97	
Jun	295	361	7	190	--	--	16	2	61	180	
TOTAL	3,103	5,224	93	5,073	2,031	79	224F 196m	19	798	1,043	1 GEN.

	Holdings--Start of Year	Acquired	Withdrew	Net Difference	Holdings--End of Year
paper pieces	41,287	3,103	5,073	- 1,970	39,317
microfiche cards	25,218	5,224	2,031	+ 3,193	28,441
microfilm reels	769	--	--	--	769
titles cataloged	4,596	93	79	+ 14	4,610
volumes stored	428	--	428	- 428	-0-
item numbers selected	1,335 of 6,509 (20.51%)				1,380 of 6,822 (20.23%)

SERIALS

<u>PERIODICALS</u>

Current Titles	1,539
Titles added	0
Titles cancelled	56
Total Periodical Titles in Collection	2,084

<u>NEWPAPERS</u>

Current Titles	33
Titles added	0
Titles cancelled	0
Total Newspaper Titles in Collection	48

<u>NON-PRINT FORMAT</u>

Microfilm volumes added	178
Microfilm reels added	233
Periodicals 150	
Newspapers 83	
Microfiche volumes added	457
Microfiche pieces added	4,208

<u>PRESERVATION</u>

Periodical titles bound for first time	35
Periodical titles on Microfiche first time	22
Periodical titles on Microfilm first time	0
Books Bound	175
Periodical bound	1,259
Periodical volumes withdrawn	0
TOTAL on shelf -Bound Volumes	40,508

<u>OFFICE ACTIVITY</u>

Periodicals checked in	18,401
Serials checked in	3,507
Inquiries Desk - 2276	
Fiche/film - 2697	
Phone - 597	5,570
Table of Contents Copied	1,534

<u>BUDGET</u>

	Allocation	Expenditures	Balance
Serials	$200,200.00	$216,051.73	-$15,851.73
Preservation	$18,000.00	$18,009.28	-$9.28

We sold $558.24 in back issues
We took in $1,964.60 on Microfiche and film copies

OBERLIN COLLEGE LIBRARY

Annual Report 1986-87

Oberlin College

Format:

Paper size and weight: 8.5" x 11.0"; 20 lb. bond

Cover size and weight: 8.5" x 11.0"; 80 lb. offset

B/W text; beige cover with black type and graphics

Binding: side-stitch

Production:

Editor: Shelby Warrens

Graphics designer: Shelby Warrens

Duplicated on library photocopy equipment

Number of pages: 10 (excluding covers)

Number of copies printed: 250

Stand-alone publication

Distribution:

Sent to College president, chief academic officer, vice presidents, deans, directors of other units on campus, library staff, library advisory committee, faculty, consortia libraries

Disseminated by campus mail and as a library handout

1986–87

ANNUAL REPORT
OF THE
DIRECTOR OF LIBRARIES

OBERLIN

To: S. Frederick Starr   Date: 30 June 1987
           President

From: William A. Moffett   Re: Report for 1986-87
           Director of Libraries

For the past several years, in summarizing for you the comprehensive report that is filed each year at this time in the library office, I have made reference to the plan for the eighties which has guided us throughout this decade.

This year it seems especially fitting that we look back beyond that plan to the objectives and accomplishments of Oberlin's first professional librarian, the redoubtable Azariah Smith Root. Both in reviewing our work of the past year and in looking to the future we have many occasions to recall him with a renewed sense of appreciation.

THE CATALOG, THE STAFF, STUDENT WORKERS

It was a century ago this year that the Oberlin faculty invited Root to assume the responsibilities of librarian. He had already interrupted his law studies once before at the invitation of his alma mater--he had graduated with the class of 1884--to undertake the cataloging of the books owned by the college library and the even larger collections of the students' own literary societies. He had done so, typically, after a comprehensive study of New England practices and a study of the new scheme developed by Melvil Dewey. His work had made such a favorable impression that on February 3, 1887--his twenty-fifth birthday--he was asked to give up his place at the Harvard Law School and come back once again, this time on a permanent appointment. In April he returned to Ohio, married his Elyria classmate Anna Metcalf, and broke ground in an apple orchard on North Professor Street for the home in which they were to live for forty years.

The faculty had already recorded their "great satisfaction" with the manner in which he had performed the cataloging task. According to their formal minute: "They appreciate the care with which he prepared himself for the work, and the fidelity and success with which it has been prosecuted. Mr. Root has much exceeded the terms of his contract, and made a substantial and lasting contribution to the intellectual resources of the College." That care and fidelity would consistently characterize the subsequent work of developing the remarkable catalog that emerged as Root created by 1910 the largest academic library in Ohio, and what was at that time the nineteenth largest academic library in the Republic.

Not only did he bring his own great intellect and energy to the work, he saw from the first that his was a teaching role, one which led naturally to the formation of a "library club" for members of his staff. "Once each week, in the evening," he recorded, "they meet for an hour to compare notes, to make reports on topics especially assigned, and to carry on definite courses of study." In 1899 the special topics were bibliography and cataloging; in 1900 "the general subject of library science alternates with the study and cataloging of fifteenth century books." Although for many years he was the sole professional librarian, he extended his effectiveness by seeing to the training of a strong supporting staff. Moreover, he soon introduced into the staff a number of student apprentices who were given practical training,

OBERLIN COLLEGE LIBRARY • OBERLIN, OHIO 44074

Main Library   Art Library   Science Library   Conservatory Library
The Mudd Center   Allen Art Building   Kettering Hall   Conservatory of Music
216/775-8285   216/775-8635   216/775-8310   216/775-8280

114

who attended his course in bibliography--he was made Professor of Bibliography in 1890--and joined with the staff in the discussions and work of the Library Club, all valuable experiences for whose who were interested in adopting librarianship as a life's work. "The work of training these apprentices is considerable," he noted in his annual report of that year, "but in return we receive, especially in cataloguing, extra help without which it would be impossible to keep up with the growth of the library."

For much of 1986-87 the librarian and his staff were preoccupied with completing the task of converting the card catalog--including bibliographic records written out in Root's own unmistakable hand--to machine readable form, and to negotiating a contract with Geac Computers that would enable us finally to abandon Root's card files for an online system.

In nothing did we seem so clearly to be making a dramatic break with the past. And yet, in the care and intelligence they displayed, and in their readiness to exploit new technology, Lois Lindberg, Alan Boyd, Katie Frohmberg, Ray English and their colleagues were remarkably faithful to Root's own example. Indeed, while some might harbor a nostalgic attachment to the old drawers of cards, we cannot imagine anyone who would have been more of an enthusiast for the change than Professor Root himself, or more eager for the new efficiencies and improved access the online system will bring in the coming year.

Taking a cue from Root, our approach to automation over the past decade has been a team effort in the best tradition of his "Library Club." The staff generally has joined in workshops and training sessions, in site visits and vendor presentations, in preparing our Request for Proposal for prospective vendors and in analyzing and assessing the responses. In reaching a decision to purchase the Geac 9000 system, and in negotiating with Geac officials, the director was able to draw upon unusually well-informed and sophisticated colleagues.

And we, too, like Root, are especially mindful of the special contribution made in recent years by our student apprentices. It is still quite true that without them we could not carry on the work of the library, for it has been the contribution by the student work force that has enabled us to handle a steadily increasing number of transactions, create new programs in preservation, and deal with increases in acquisitions without increasing the size of the professional staff. Indeed, given the size and complexity of the Oberlin College Libraries, we have a proportionately smaller staff than the colleges with whom we compare ourselves.

As it was for Root, it is in the cataloging department that the student contribution has been most signficant. Over the five year project to convert all our old bibliographic records to a machine-readable format, we have employed well over a hundred different students at computer terminals and related tasks for over 23,700 hours--the equivalent of the annual workload of a dozen full-time staffers. By using this workforce we were able to convert our records at $1.12 a title, nearly half the unit cost experienced by academic libraries nationally, and completed the project at a record pace.

We have, moreover, continued Professor Root's practice of regarding student jobs as opportunities for learning. We have taken seriously our responsibilities as teachers. We have been instrumental in clarifying for students the challenges of librarianship as a profession, and gratified to find some of our best student assistants going into it. This year, for the first time, one of our Metcalf Student Assistants (Anne Zald '82) emerged from a national search as our top choice for a professional appointment, giving us an Oberlin grad on the staff after many many years and reviving a tradition that began with Root himself.

ACQUISITIONS FUNDING

The most persistent theme of Professor Root's annual reports was the insufficiency of the funds available for acquiring library materials. An 1894 report on the paucity of funds allotted him is characteristic: "The utter inadequacy of this is too obvious to need mentioning. With the very modest salaries paid in Oberlin, there is a more imperative need for book-funds than there would be in richer institutions. We must provide for the corps of instruction, as well as for the student body, those books which will stimulate thought and keep it abreast of modern movements." And in 1902: "For many departments, the library is truly the laboratory; and the courses can as little be rightly conducted without these indispensable books as a laboratory course could be g iven without apparatus." He constantly urged successive presidents to increase allocations and worked to build up the library endowment. In 1925 he was instrumental in getting what was at that time an unprecedented gift to the College of $50,000 from the Carnegie Corporation, the entire income of which was added to the appropriation for books, "the faculty almost unanimously feeling that this was the greatest need of the Library."

In 1986-87 Root's successor was sounding the same theme. For years the compounding effects of cuts in the acquisitions budget made in 1973-74 had crippled collection development and thrust Oberlin to the very bottom of the scale of acquisitions funding among leading colleges. In 1982 college administrators had agreed that funding comparable at least to what had existed in 1973 must be restored, but after initial increases the fulfillment of the pledge slowed to a crawl. In 1986 Oberlin still ranked near the bottom of its peers in dollars spent per student on library materials and in December the faculty committee felt compelled to bring a resolution to the general faculty expressing concern and urging the administration to fulfill the pledge as quickly as possible. It received unanimous approval. The Provost subsequently took steps to facilitate access to income from recent additions to the endowment and gave assurances that fulfillment of the pledge was still a top priority. The approved budget for 1987-88 projects yet another installment, still some $40,000 short of the target but with good reason to think that we will have at least regained the 1973 threshold before the end of the eighties. In the meantime the drawn-out process will have cost the library's collections the benefit of nearly half a million dollars that might have been ours had the pledge been immediately redeemed in full, and leaves Oberlin still well down the list. We think we know what Azariah Root would say.

The situation is made even more acute by recent substantial increases in the prices of scholarly journals--especially in the sciences--a crisis made worse by the decline of the dollar overseas. Our subscription costs rose sharply this past year, well ahead of the rate of increase in the acquisitions budget. In 1987-88, as it was for Professor Root a century ago, our most worrying concern is sure to be the problem of having enough dollars to purchase the materials needed to support Oberlin faculty's needs.

FRIENDS, TEACHING THE HISTORY OF THE BOOK

"From the very beginning," Root's daughter Polly was to recall in a memoir she prepared in 1955, "ASR apparently realized that the Oberlin College Library must secure much of its material by gift, and he encouraged gifts in every possible way." In many of the early years about a third of the new accessions came by gift, with a large store of duplicates accumulating which eventually brought in many valuable additions as exchanges with other libraries. Even in 1922, when he added in one year almost as many bound volumes as Oberlin had owned when he became librarian thirty-five years before, over half came by gift.

In his 1911 report he noted: "During the year one of our professors who has been preparing a work for publication has again and again spoken to me with delight of unusual books which he had not been able to find in some of the large libraries of the world but which he found in our collection, the gift of some friend of bygone years. It is, of course, difficult always to forecast what any subsequent generation of students and investigators is likely to desire but I have more and more frequent evidence of the wisdom of the policy hitherto pursued by the library in encouraging gifts and adding material which, at the time, seemed of comparatively little value. I trust that the stream of gifts which for these many years has so greatly enriched our collections may grow broader and richer as the years go on." In a later report Root added: "To one who has been receiving ...gifts for more than twenty-five years the wonder ever grows that a community no larger than Oberlin should year after year send such a steady flow of books into the library and that so many of them should prove valued additions."

In 1917 he observed: "We are adding pretty largely books of current origin. Obviously, a library which is to be for research workers must include as well the literature of earlier centuries. Every early printed book, every 16th century pamphlet, every book which marks an epoch in the scholarship of any given field adds to the ability of the library to trace the development of knowledge." He confessed that though "we ought to purchase more of this older material," Oberlin's "main dependence must be upon those who have these older books, which are becoming too expensive to be bought with the funds available for purchases. There must be among our graduates and among friends of the College many collectors of these books of earlier generations. It is to them that the library must look for its valuable additions."

In describing the gift of a Latin Bible published by Anthony Koburger of Nuremberg in 1478 as "a most welcome addition for the use of the class in the History of Printing," he added almost wistfully, "I wish some man interested in collecting examples of printing, particularly the fine printing of the present day, such as the Kelmscott Press and other private presses, could be interested to give his collection to the College."

One of the principal events of 1986-87 for us was the celebration of exactly such a gift, the library of Frederick B. Artz (1894-1983), a member of the class of 1916 and one of Oberlin's most distinguished scholar/teachers. His magnificent collection of books, maps, and other materials would have delighted Root, just as it did the hundreds of guests who visited the exhibit in the Allen Art Museum in November. The exhibit and its symposium, including one speaker (Harold Jantz '29) whose career began as an Oberlin student in the last years of Root's service, provided a fitting inauguration for The Friends of the Oberlin College Library. In May an advisory committee of alumni met in the board room of the Free Library of Philadelphia to review the rationale and governance structure of the Friends. Subsequently Erwin N. Griswold '25 agreed to act as honorary chairman of the new association, and Robert I. Rotberg '55 agreed to chair a related visiting committee. As this year ends we are working to identify a solid corps of friends and alumni who can revive and sustain Root's vision of an enriching "stream of gifts that will flow on for years to come."

At the same time we are reviving the studies in bibliography and the history of the book which Root pioneered at Oberlin, and for which our special collections are an excellent resource. In 1987-88 we hope to offer the first experimental sessions of such studies as part of a planning process for submitting a formal proposal to the appropriate faculty committee.

PHYSICAL PLANT

During Root's own college days the library, such as it was, was housed in a small brick building on campus that served as headquarters for the literary societies. At the 1884 commencement, when he graduated, it was announced that a new building was to be erected as the result of a major gift. Consequently, in 1887 Root began his career in a brand new structure. As both collection and student body grew, the Spear Library soon proved inadequate, however, and within fifteen years Root was lobbying for a new building. In 1904-05 an offer from Andrew Carnegie of a gift of $125,000 towards a new structure gave Root a unique opportunity to design a library and he made the most of it. The result, dedicated in June 1908--the address being delivered by "the accomplished librarian of Harvard University," Mr. William Coolidge Lane--was impressive for elegantly achieving his basic objectives: the best possible quarters for a library, fireproof, adequately lighted and ventilated, economical to administer, and sufficient in size to allow for growth.

Quite simply, to quote Keyes Metcalf, Root's protege and himself librarian of Harvard and the world's leading authority on library construction, "ASR planned and brought into being the finest college library building that had been produced up to that time and a building that cost less for the facilities that it gave than any other building I know of." Toward the end of his career Root was planning modular additions that would permit expansion of Carnegie in successive installments, another strikingly modern idea. Root thus demonstrated the truism that great librarians are masters of space and light as well as bibliography, that they are "buildings people" as well as "book people."

In 1986-87 buildings issues continued to be a leading concern for Root's successors. Long a showcase for visitors, the heavily used main library in Mudd is showing the inevitable signs of wear and tear. Maintenance and repair is scarcely matching the deterioration of its once bright fabrics and gleaming surfaces. An inadequate HVAC system fails to filter out dust and air-borne particulate matter--and worse, fails to control humidity. (A long delayed project to modify at least the zones governing archives and special collections has been unaccountably pushed back another year.) In the crowded branch libraries, space has run out, and in the case of the art library, at least, there is no conceivable way to expand.

The good news, of course, is that we ended this year by breaking ground for the exciting new addition for the Conservatory Library designed by Gunnar Birkerts and Associates, a structure that will ultimately triple our space there. We have been encouraged by the responsiveness of the firm to our concerns and suggestions. Much of the coming year will be devoted, in collaboration with the new conservatory librarian, Daniel Zager, to the refinement of the interior designs, the selection of furnishings, and planning the refurbishing of the existing facility. The chief obstacle now is that although there is sufficient funding to complete the new addition, there are as yet inadequate funds with which to refurbish the older part, including the listening area which is one of the major objectives of the expansion project. If the development office is successful in obtaining the assistance of major donors, or if the trustees authorize other funds, it should be possible to move into the new quarters during next summer and dedicate the refurbished and extended library by the opening of the fall term, 1988.

Scarcely less interesting, especially in the context of this report, is the intention of the college administration to return the second floor reading room of Carnegie, as well as the stacks formerly reserved for the Oberlin Public Library, to the jurisdiction of the Oberlin College Library, preserving the option of future consolidation there of our various holdings and services in support of the natural sciences. In 1987-88 we will attempt to insure that the timetable for the Carnegie renovations provides for early restoration of the reading room and the essential conversion of the ventilation system of the Carnegie stacks according to standards acceptable for archival purposes.

LIBRARY SERVICE TO THE COMMUNITY

It seemed natural enough to Root to extend library service to the entire community, especially at a time when distinctions between "town" and "gown" were frequently blurred. (Root himself was for many years president of the Board of Education; he served as both secretary and president of the Board of Commerce; was a director of the Oberlin Telephone Company; director and president of the Oberlin Mutual Benefit Association; secretary of the local Board of Health; member of the Water Works Inspection Committee; active in the Village Improvement Society; chaired various committees in the First Church of Oberlin, served as superintendent of the Sunday School, taught Bible classes and regularly preached in the town's black churches.) He opened Spear library to adult readers on a basis restricted primarily by the specialized nature of the collection and the limited space of the reading room.

When the possibility of a new college library to replace Spear first came into view Professor Root proposed that, under an existing Ohio law, the college enter into a contract with the local board of education whereby the facilities of the college library should be made available to the citizens of the town in consideration of a one-mill tax levy. Since he was at the time president of the board, it was not difficult to effect the agreement. Thus began an unorthodox arrangement, typically Oberlinian, that led the college to provide special library assistance to the community for nearly eighty years. Three first-floor rooms were designated for public use, one as a children's room and two as popular reading and reference rooms. The money received from the town was spent, half for salaries of attendants and half for the purchase of books for the open shelf and children's rooms; townspeople were able to withdraw books from the college's general collection and take advantage of the services of the reference librarian, while the arrangement also served to provide books of fiction, biography, travel and other general interest materials for students and faculty. It also provided a place in which town and gown could come together, a matter of great concern to Root who took an active interest in the town's affairs and worked diligently to insure friendly relations.

If Azariah Root were alive in 1986-87 he would undoubtedly support the re-affirmation of the special relationship between the college and the town in the matter of the library. The president of the college has given assurances that the college is prepared to assist the trustees of the Oberlin Public Library in securing a new home. He has asked the director of libraries to help represent the college in the joint effort to plan and locate a new public library building that will insure improved service to the entire community. In undertaking that commission, he will find the example of Professor Root instructive and to the point.

NATIONAL AND REGIONAL LEADERSHIP

Although Root had more than enough to keep him busy in Oberlin, he did not fail to contribute to the wider library community. Even during the hectic year of 1907-08, which involved moving the library into its new quarters, he was overseeing the creation of an Ohio union list of periodicals. "It is hoped by this means to save the smaller libraries from the expense involved in collecting the less frequently used sets, to increase interlibrary loans, and to relieve the larger libraries outside the state from the many calls upon their good nature and generosity." The next year, and in the years following, he was advocating the advantages of greater co-ordination among libraries, of creating a clearinghouse for the exchange of duplicates, of central storage facilities for little-used books, of creating strong regional libraries, of collaborative collection development by neighboring libraries, and of ways of improving the creation of printed catalog cards--all pioneering ideas which were eventually adopted by the profession.

He served as a member of the faculty of the School of Library Science of Western Reserve University from its founding until his death in 1927, making the two-hour journey to Cleveland one day a week for ten weeks each year to lecture on the history of printing and the book arts. He regularly lectured at the University of Michigan, the library school of the Pratt Institute in Brooklyn, the library school of The New York Public Library (which he served as acting director during 1916-17), and at Chautauqua. He was especially active in efforts on the part of the American Library Association to improve the training of librarians.

In 1901-02 he served as president of the Ohio Library Association and as chairman of the College Section of the American Library Association; he was an early member of the Bibliographical Society of America and served as its president in 1910-11 and again in 1924-26. He served on a number of key committees of the American Library Association and in 1922 was elected its president--one of only three college librarians ever to hold that office. His presidential address emphasized the need for more efficient library administration, for greater standardization of methodology (so that energy would be saved for the more important work of "making our libraries an effective force for transforming their communities"), and above all for an end to provincialism and lack of cooperation: "The great need of American libraries today is that each library should think not in terms of itself and its own interests, but in the spirit and conception of library unity. Each must be ready to give and each ready to take whatever action will be for the greatest good of all our American libraries." It was the Oberlin experience proposed as a national plan.

It still falls to the Oberlin librarian to participate widely in both state and national library matters, and to attempt to provide leadership where that seems appropriate. Though no longer the largest academic library in Ohio, Oberlin continues to play a leading role in such state-wide efforts as the campaign to establish a cooperative preservation agency; our professional staff are active in the Academic Library Association of Ohio, chairing committees and offering workshops; we are an essential partner in NEOMARL, the consortium of major academic and research libraries in northeastern Ohio.

In 1987, for example, we spearheaded an effort to improve interlibrary lending through telefacsimile transmission of documents, and agreed to be project director of a federal grant which, if authorized, would not only provide fax equipment and supplies to NEOMARL members but promote its use and support the study of its impact during 1987-88.

In November 1986 we hosted the first national conference of college librarians, convening at Oberlin the heads of the country's fifty leading independent liberal arts college libraries for two very productive days of discussion. The experiment proved highly successful and the "Oberlin group" seems likely to become a continuing informal association. It will meet for its second annual retreat in October 1987 at Grinnell to take up proposals for joint efforts first developed here last fall.

The director of libraries has been a visible presence in national academic library affairs. He serves on the editorial board of the **Journal of Academic Librarianship** and the college and university advisory committee of OCLC. He is active in the Association of College and Research Libraries--the outgrowth of the College Section of the ALA of which Azariah Root was an early chairman. He has recently concluded a three-year term on the executive board of the college libraries section, currently chairs a major committee of the rare books and manuscripts section, is liaison to the British rare books group of the Library Association (U.K.), will present a major program at the 1988 New Orleans meeting of the American Library Association, and has accepted nomination as a candidate for the presidency of the ACRL in the 1988 elections.

THE ROLE OF THE COLLEGE LIBRARIAN AT OBERLIN

Azariah Root died on October 2, 1927 of heart failure following an operation. Years later Keyes Metcalf remembered him as one of the truly vital members of the Oberlin faculty: "He in some way or other contrived to make the library the real center of the college life. This was not only because of the collection and the building, but the service given and his personal influence on faculty and students. ASR was without doubt the most influential member of the faculty of his time, and his administrative ability was used to a very great extent again and again; it had a great deal to do with making Oberlin one of the top colleges in the country. He played an important part in academic freedom during the World War years; he was an unusually fine speaker and a great teacher, and in those two ways impressed his personality and his profession on a great many people throughout the country, in libraries and elsewhere."

Another protege wrote: "Professor Root was, I suspect, one of the most loved members of the faculty among the students. Many thought of him, I'm sure, as a personal friend. Of course in the earlier days he did the 'reference work,' seeming to know just what any questioner needed and where to find it--this in a day when there were not the indexes and other aids that developed later. But he was as willing to notice and help a youngster, a high school freshman, as he was in pointing out sources to a college senior. He believed that students should learn early how to approach a large library collection independently using the tools for guidance, but it is still heart-warming to remember the way in which he would come to a table himself (even when there was an excellent, friendly reference librarian on duty) with arms filled with books for the searcher... He had a broad view of a library's function in a college. He had vision for the book collection and the services to be given students and the entire community. To these ends he devoted an intellect of superior drive and originality. Petty things didn't worry him. He had confidence in his staff and believed that staff members had discretion and training to handle difficulties within the range of their authority... I never had a more encouraging supervisor."

Root was chairman of the budget committee of the college for many years, and a member of the prudential committee for nearly thirty-five years; he served long terms as vice-chairman of the general faculty, the college faculty, and the general council. From 1906 to his death he was chairman of the boarding halls committee; he served on the committee on honorary degrees, preparing the citations and presenting the candidates at a number of commencements. One of his first non-library assignments--in 1894--had been to prepare for publication the Quinquennial Catalogue, a 200-page volume containing the address of every graduate, and subsequently he was a member of the committee on supervision of appeals to alumni and the committee on alumni relations. For much of 1901-02 he was busy as chair of the committee canvassing funds to enable the college to meet the provision of John D. Rockefeller's conditional gift, in which capacity he went personally to any area in which the campaign was not being pushed successfully--resulting in the addition of $500,000 to the funds of the college.

He served on committees on the relation to the town and the environment, on intercollegiate debate, on student publications and public exercises, on monthly lectures. He was for many years the secretary of the college and during two academic years served as acting president for Henry Churchill King (1909-10 and 1925-26). In the review of his first such experience, he included in his comprehensive report an analysis of the situation regarding white and black students--a disturbing issue that year, and asserted on behalf of the faculty its conviction "that the fundamental principle of the brotherhood of men, of all classes and color, which has been the Oberlin pride for more than seventy-five years, is based upon such fundamental principles of righteousness and justice that it must in the long run command the assent of thoughtful students."

One of the Trustees wrote Mrs. Root after his death: "He was such a broad-minded man, so tolerant, so enthusiastic, so hard-working, so appreciative of big things and yet so willing to do the little things that must be done to keep matters going smoothly, that he combined an unusual number of rare qualities. I used to think of him somewhat as a Benjamin Franklin, for among other things he was very wise."

In February 1987 we marked the centenary of Azariah Smith Root's appointment as librarian at Oberlin. In October we observe the sixtieth anniversary of his death. In this year, and for many years to come, his life of service will both inspire and measure the work of his successors.

WAM/slw

BOATWRIGHT MEMORIAL LIBRARY

Annual Report 1986-1987

within Annual Report of the President 1987

University of Richmond

Format:

Paper size and weight: 8.5" x 11.0"; 60 lb. offset

Cover size and weight: 8.5" x 11.0"; 65 lb. Cover stock

B/W cover and text

Binding: hot glue

Production:

Editors: Dr. John A. Roush, Executive Assistant to the President, and Ada C. Johnson, Secretary to Dr. Roush

Graphics designer: Walter von Klein, Registrar

Printed by the University print shop; offset

Number of pages (library report): 3

Number of copies printed: 275

Published as a section of the University President's annual report

Distribution:

Sent to board of trustees, president, chief academic officer, vice presidents, deans, directors of other campus units, chairman of university senate, library staff, library advisory committee, faculty

Disseminated by campus mail; available to faculty upon request to the Executive Assistant to the President

UNIVERSITY OF RICHMOND
VIRGINIA
FOUNDED 1830

ANNUAL REPORT
of the President

1987

study. As in previous years, representatives from several study abroad programs and foreign universities visited the campus to share information about their programs.

Plans were made and funds were provided to implement in 1987 – 88 three important recommendations of the ad hoc International Studies Committee, established in the fall of 1983. These recommendations, contained in the Committee's 1985 report, entitled "Enhancing International Competence at the University of Richmond," are for the establishment of an Office of International Education headed by a Director, a standing Committee on International Education, and an undergraduate international studies major. Dr. Gabara has been selected as the Interim Director for the 1987 – 88 session. It is our anticipation that the Office of International Education will further enhance opportunities at the University for those interested in international studies.

THE UNIVERSITY OF RICHMOND LIBRARIES
John C. Tyson, University Librarian

This was a year of transition for the Libraries in that John Tyson was appointed University Librarian effective August 1, 1986. The Libraries made significant progress toward fulfilling several organizational goals and priorities. These goals addressed concerns regarding staffing levels, services, facilities, and new technologies that were identified shortly after the arrival of the new University Librarian. Among the significant developments initiated during the 1986 – 87 academic year were:

➤ Implementation of an on-going "Strategic Long-Range Planning" process to assist library faculty and staff in planning future programs and services. During the spring semester, all University Libraries' personnel participated in a staff development program on the mechanics of strategic long-range planning. The Libraries' personnel have already realized a return on the investment of time and energy to the process. There now exists an organizational charter for the Libraries' future in the form of a mission statement and organizational goals statements. Once fully approved and communicated, it is hoped that this charter will reflect the values and priorities of the University's administration, faculty, and students for future library services.

➤ The implementation of a "Teambuilding Program" which laid the foundation for a more cohesive workgroup and an improved organizational climate. New structures were created, particularly the Library Senate with its expanded governance role, and the Library Council, to encourage staff participation in the library-wide decision-making process. The teambuilding program facilitated the implementation of many organizational changes this year because the total group was able to plan the changes together.

➤ The reassignment of existing faculty and staff to four key positions (Director of Technical Services, Head of General Reference Department, Systems Development Librarian and Accounting Clerk). This action improved greatly management of the Libraries' existing human and financial resources.

➤ The funding of four new positions (Director of Public Services, Assistant Cataloger with responsibility for Rare Books and Special Collections, Night Supervisor, and Secretary/Receptionist) which will enable the Libraries to enhance programs and services in virtually every area of the Libraries.

➤ The May, 1987 groundbreaking for the construction of 48,000 square foot new addition to the library system's facility and the renovation of the existing structure.

➤ The appointment of a university-wide "Task Force on Library Automation" to develop specifications for an on-line integrated library automation system. The goal is to acquire a system that meets the total in-house automation requirements for the Libraries, including bibliographic file maintenance, authority, reserve, serials, and circulation control; on-line public access catalog; acquisitions; audio-visual book; and remote database communications.

➤ The acquisition of the InfoTrac system, a turnkey software/hardware data package which utilizes laser disc technology for periodical index searching and retrieval.

➤ The successful completion of three grant proposals seeking funding from outside agencies to acquire new technologies which will improve the Libraries' efficiency and effectiveness. The Libraries' faculty worked with the Director of the Office of Foundation and Government Grants on the following proposals:

• A proposal of $300,000 from the Pew Charitable Trust for a computerized, on-line catalog and circulation system to link the University's libraries.

• A proposal of $400,000 to assist with construction costs for the enlarged Business Information Center to be housed in the new addition to Boatwright Library.

• A proposal to the Virginia State Library to participate in a "Document Delivery Among Multitype Library Institutions Using Telefacsimile Transmission" project to be funded through U. S. Department of Education, under Title III funds. ($48,705)

ORGANIZATION

Improvements in the University Libraries' services and in management of their human resources have been made possible through several changes in the organizational structure and staffing patterns. As of January 5, 1987, the University Libraries adopted a new organizational structure, which includes the following changes:

➤ The creation of a Public Services Division which will strengthen the Libraries' public service programs. The position of Director of Public Services will coordinate library activities in the areas of reference, library instruction, circulation, government documents, collection development, reserves, interlibrary loan, security, and stack maintenance.

The creation of a Technical Services Division with four discrete departments: The Acquisitions Department, the Cataloging Department, the Serials Department, and Systems Development. The Director of Technical Services will coordinate activities in the areas of cataloging, acquisitions, serials, gifts and exchange, and systems development. The Systems Development Librarian, a newly created position within this division, is responsible for initiating and coordinating the development and implementation of automated systems for the main and branch libraries.

Two advisory bodies to the University Librarian were created, the Library Senate and the Library Council. The Library Senate is composed of library faculty with major responsibility for the cost centers administered by the University Librarian. It consists of the Director of Public Services, Director of Technical Services, Director of the Learning Resources Center, the Business Librarian, Music Librarian, and Science Librarian. The Library Senate serves as the policy making body for University Libraries. The Library Council is composed of seven members (three library faculty and four operating staff) elected from the eligible members of the Libraries' faculty and staff holding regular employment contracts with the University. Council members are elected for two year terms and are responsible for advising the University Librarian in the areas of personnel recruitment, selection, retention, and staff development.

COLLECTIONS

The collections of the Libraries, which support both current programs of instruction and research on this campus, rank among the strongest in the state. According to data regarding "volumes held" provided by the State Council on Higher Education in Virginia (SCHEV), as of June 30, 1986, the University of Richmond Libraries ranked second among the 33 reporting libraries in private institutions in Virginia and ranked eighth among all 72 academic libraries in Virginia. The Libraries provide access not only to the 725,000 items (books, microforms, periodicals, films, tapes, slides, maps, etc.) housed at the University but also to the library resources of other institutions throughout the state and nation via interlibrary loan services.

The Libraries received several notable gifts this year. They were the William Trousdale Allen Collection (147 discs); the Clarke Bustard Collection (99 discs); the David John Mays Collection of Famous American Cartoons (50 vols.); The George F. Scheer Collection of University Press Books (42 vols.); and the William Dew Gresham Collection of World Literature (1,250 vols.). The Gresham Collection is especially noteworthy, as the potential basis of a local center for literary research using signed, numbered, first editions. The collection is valued at more than $30,000 and will be housed in the Rare Book Room.

FACILITIES

Extensive renovation of the existing Boatwright Memorial Library facility and construction of a four-story addition began in May, 1987. The 48,000 square foot structure will be on the west side of the existing building, and will add approximately 30,000 square feet of finished library space, 8,000 square feet of unfinished space, and 10,000 square feet for the housing of the Lora Robins Gallery (a rock and gem museum). It is anticipated that the construction will be completed in 18 months (October, 1988). The new addition will offer greatly improved library facilities to staff and library patrons, and the renovated areas will enable the Libraries to better utilize existing space in the building.

PERSONNEL

New Appointments

Paul Porterfield, Director, Learning Resources Center

Melanie Hillner, Science Librarian

Lucretia McCulley, Reference Librarian

John Walters, Reference/Government Documents Librarian

Leigh McDonald, Cataloging Librarian

Paul Duffy, Library Assistant, Night Supervisor

Iria Jones, Library Specialist, Acquisitions/Cataloging Department

Robert Jones, Library Clerk, Serials Department

Fenton Shugrue, Library Assistant, Government Documents Department

Promotions

James Gwin, Head of Cataloging to Director, Technical Services Division

Kate DuVal, Collection Development Librarian to Head, General Reference Department and Acting Director, Public Services Division

Lila Williams, Cataloging Librarian to Systems Development Librarian

Lynda Jenkins, Library Specialist to Library Assistant and Coordinator of Acquisitions

Peggy Sutherland, Library Clerk to Library Specialist, Acquisitions Department

Mary Beth Bartlow, Library Clerk to Library Specialist, Cataloging Department

Reassignments

James Gwin, Head, Cataloging Department to Acting Director, Learning Resources Center (July – December, 1986)

Christine Campbell, Half-time Cataloging Librarian to Half-time Reference Librarian

Beth Stiegler, Full-time Library Specialist to Half-time Library Specialist, Cataloging Department

Carol Sutton-Abaire, Library Assistant, Acquisitions Department to Accounting Clerk, Library Administration

Resignations

Patricia Gregory, Head, General Reference Department

Isabel Paul, Government Documents Librarian

Rebecca Garrison, Library Specialist, Cataloging Department

Patricia Willis, Library Specialist, Circulation Department

Katherine Smith, Science Librarian: During Ms. Smith's 15 years of service, she made an extraordinary contribution in directing the growth of the Science Library's collection and its outstanding service programs.

GENERAL STATISTICS
July 1, 1986 — June 30, 1987

Acquisitions — Print	'85 – 86	'86 – 87
Books		
Purchased	13,601	11,637
Gifts	1,353	1,695
Government Documents — Print	13,762	8,526
Government Documents — Microform	14,372	16,495
Microforms	3,480	2,485
Bound Periodicals	2,025	2,240
Current Periodicals Added	57	40

Acquisitions — Nonprint		
Films (16mm & 8mm)	4	5
Filmstrips — Cassettes	0	0
Audio Tapes — Cassettes	175	0
Video Tapes — Purchased	25	235
Sound Recordings — Spoken Arts	0	0
Slides (Series)	1	0
Slide/tapes	0	0
Maps	0	2
Kits	15	0

Cataloging		
Volumes Cataloged	13,352	12,598
Volumes Recataloged — Dewey	461	492
Volumes Recataloged — L.C.	663	904
Sound Recordings — Music	386	274
Sound Recordings Reclass (Music Library)	99	45
Audio Cassettes	175	83
Video Cassettes	85	265
Kits	15	3
Filmstrips	20	3
Slides	80	48
Motion Pictures (16mm)	10	3
Periodical Volumes Cataloged	220	144
Computer Software Cataloged	9	5
CD/ROM Cataloged	0	204
Books Lost	449	258
Books Found	0	19
Books Withdrawn	1,314	641
Government Documents Withdrawn	1,050	1,525
Government Documents Withdrawn (Microfiche)	200	1,728
Graduate Theses Cataloged	7	24

Circulation		
Volumes Borrowed	52,175	44,809
Reserve Borrowing	20,855	20,775

Interlibrary Loan		
Items Borrowed	1,316	1,
Items Loaned	4,063	4,
On-line Computer Literature Searches	562	

LRC Media Statistics		
Media Rented	241	
Media Loaned to Co-op Members	601	
Media Borrowed from Co-op Members	700	

Total Collections As Of June 30, 1987

	'85 – 86	'86
Books & Bound Volumes (Excluding Law, Gov. Documents)	334,402	346,
Government Documents	178,142	185,
Government Documents — Microform	126,233	141,
Periodical Subscriptions	3,189	3,
Microforms	24,016	26,
Films	420	
Filmstrips	292	
Audio/Tape/Cassettes	1,416	1,
Video Tape	488	
Sound Recordings — Spoken Arts	699	
Sound Recordings — Music	9,380	9,
CD/ROM — Music	12	
Slides	9,380	9,
Kits	77	

UNIVERSITY COLLEGE
Max Graeber, Dean

The four areas of University College and their impact on University and the area are listed below.

1. Summer School *class enrollments*

Six Sessions	2,146	
Masters, Business Administration	(187)†	
T. C. Williams Law School	(117)†	
Total		2,14

†Numbers in ( ) not included in UC totals.

2. Evening School *class enrollments*

Fall and Spring Sessions	1,751	
Total		1,75

3. Women's Resource Center

Courses, workshops, support groups, career counseling, peer counseling, and legal information services, plus lunch programs, speeches, and programs given by staff members	6,106	
Total		6,1

WOLFGRAM MEMORIAL LIBRARY

Annual Report 1985-1986

within President's Report 1985-1986

Widener University

Format:

Paper size and weight: 8.5" x 11.0"; 60 lb. white smooth offset

Cover size and weight: 8.5" x 11.0"; cream white Line stock

B/W cover type and picture; royal blue square (surrounding picture) and bar (foot margin) on cover; B/W contents except for the royal blue section headline ("The Libraries" plus the underscore), and three royal blue subsection headings: "Pennsylvania Campus," "Delaware Campus," "Law Library"

Binding: saddle-stitch

Production:

Editor: Mary Anderson, Office of University Relations

Printed offset commercially

Number of pages (library report): 4

Number of copies: 5,500

Published as a section of the University President's annual report

Distribution:

Sent to board of trustees, president, chief academic officer, vice presidents, deans, directors of campus units, faculty, donors

Disseminated by Office of University relations via campus mail and U.S.P.S.

PRESIDENT'S REPORT
1985-1986

UNIVERSITY

We take your education personally.

THE LIBRARIES

The Wolfgram Memorial Library is continuing to make measurable prog collection building, the improvement and marketing of existing services, access to outside resources, planning toward the necessary enhancement facilities, and the adaptation of modern technologies.

SERVICES Traditional reference services are now enhanced by various technologies. A microcomputer permits the reference librarians to search commercial databases at lower cost, printing the results of searches inhou thus eliminating the time needed for delivery. New rates for "after dark" access to a number of services have attracted the user for whom the cost formation retrieval may have been a deterrent. Interlibrary loan procedu with the help of a new computer program, can handle the increasing nun requests more efficiently. Additionally, more user-oriented nonprint servi have been selected, e.g., InfoTrac, a computer-accessed laser disc index, public terminal for OCLC, the nationwide union catalog, both identifying graphic records.

The *Workbook,* to instruct freshmen on how to use an academic libr has been revised and its testing methods made more reliable.

In recognition of the excellence of the library's *User Guide,* its revised was given a Certificate of Merit by ALA's Library Public Relations Cou

COLLECTION The stronger book budget allowed us to continue the acce collection building program. The work of liaison librarians helped increa faculty awareness of available well-reviewed publications. Attention was to the obsolescence of certain reference materials, and a "deselection pr gram" of superseded titles has been initiated. New titles were added esp in support of graduate programs. In order to meet the need for a balance lection adapted to Widener's academic priorities, the Collection Develop Policy was formulated. This document will serve as a valuable tool to fa and administration in the materials selection process.

With the better access to bibliographic information, we are using sul tially more outside resources, especially through interlibrary loan.

AUDIOVISUAL SERVICES Acquisition of audiovisual materials also a healthy increase. Liaison work with faculty and the team work of all r administrators on campus resulted in effective selection decisions and in a collection with an over-20 percent circulation growth. Lower purchase c videotapes, and lease arrangements make some more permanently useful terials available on campus. The head of Audiovisual Services continues efforts to develop shared media resources for our consortia and for departmental collections on both campus. A computer produced audiovisual software catalog was recently completed.

A special endowment, through the Geoghegan Fund, is enabling us to establish a compact disc collection for classical and American music. Purchase of equipment and of a core collection is underway. Continuous funding will make the growth of this collection possible.

PERSONNEL Continuing education and training increased the technical skills of staff members. Introductory and advanced workshops for the library's micros and specific software capabilities are bringing us to various levels of mastery.

All librarians and some support staff participated in the Association of College and Research Libraries biennial conference in Baltimore. Workshops on supervision, automation, new techniques for bibliographic instruction, use and usefulness of consultants, fund raising and research opportunities were taken.

Four members of the library staff reached the landmarks of 10, 15, and 20 years of service to Widener. We also lost some valuable and respected staff members including our archivist emeritus who retired from her second career at the library.

The assistant director for Technical and Automated Services was elected to OCLC's User Council, a national advisory group. The director is one of the regional representatives for the Association of College and Research Libraries' College Library Section and also trustee of the Crozer Lewis Library in Chester. Our senior secretary is trustee of the Lansdowne Public Library.

AUTOMATION With the acquisition of specialized equipment, the database search operation was transformed into one of higher efficiency and lower cost with more potential for direct use by students and faculty. Planning and studying of available and rapidly developing computer technologies have resulted in the decision to replace the book acquisitions system on the Burroughs with Bib/Base Acq. which will be installed in 1986-87. The ROM terminal, used to verify student records this past year, has proven to be a great help in identifying the validity of user privileges and has enhanced our ability to retrieve borrowed material.

Public services benefit from a new computer-produced union list of audiovisual materials and a pamphlet catalog.

FURNISHING AND EQUIPMENT Capital funds made the purchase of additional microform reader and copying equipment possible. Some new furnishing, to house micro and other office equipment, cabinets, chairs and tables, the repair of lounge chairs, and the purchase of study chairs will enhance user comfort.

PLANS, NEEDS ASSESSMENTS A major self-study focused on the library building. The resulting report addressed space problems, increased student population, a growing collection, and new technologies. Plans to better utilize the fourth floor now serving as storage area, and to relocate some nonlibrary services, address the space needs anticipated by the move of the School of Hotel and Restaurant Management to this campus. Liaison work to move some of the collection from the Delaware Campus and to budget for the special materials and additional library services needed for this program are being coordinated by the assistant director for public services.

DELAWARE CAMPUS

The Thanksgiving holiday of 1985 brought a true sense of thankfulness from the students, faculty and staff of the Delaware Campus because of the completion of the new library addition. New furnishings and refurbishings, a well-defined front entrance, an open spaciousness in the reference area, a quiet study nook, plenty of seating spaces, and the ending of all construction noise, dust and dirt, were deeply appreciated by all. A much needed facility had been added for all the Delaware Campus to enjoy.

SERVICES On November 11, 1985, the Delaware Campus Library staff started moving into the new addition. With the help of work-study students and volunteer classes from the Liberal Arts and Fashion Merchandising Departments, the complete collection was reshelved in approximately 35 hours. The move was essentially completed on November 17.

The new addition provides some 50 percent increased capacity, and adds a new Reference and Information Service Office, a Media Center, the director's

office, a conference room, two compact storage facilities, a multi-media area and a quiet reading loft. The new facility also has display cases and standing panels suitable for art and photographic displays.

The InfoTrac database system is a new service added to the Delaware Campus Library in late January. This system contains references to articles from approximately 1,000 business, technical and general interest publication This new service harnesses the latest in technology to provide the student wi effective, low-cost access to current bibliographic information.

Interlibrary loans continued to grow as a greater number of the library's catalog records were entered in OCLC, the international library database. T of the most frequent borrowers from out-of-state were the Brookings Institut Library in Washington, D.C. and the U.S. Naval Library at Patuxent, Mary land. Loans were made to such diverse institutions as San Jose University Library in California, the British Library Lending Division in Yorkshire, England, and the Smithsonian Institution in Washington, D.C.

PERSONNEL Jane E. Hukill, director of the Delaware Campus Library, w the speaker for the Associated College Libraries of Central Pennsylvania at annual spring meeting at Susquehanna University. Her topic was "Does the Accreditation Process Really Work for Libraries?" Mrs. Hukill also served president of the Tri-State College Library Consortium during this past year.

AUTOMATION The Delaware Campus Library completed the retrospecti conversion of 13,503 bibliographic records into machine-readable format. Th was accomplished with an LSCA grant provided through the Delaware Divis of Libraries. The library should now be able to proceed with the Delaware Law School Library to establish a union list of holdings for the Delaware Campus.

AUDIOVISUAL The new Media Center opened in November upon compl tion of the new library addition. New services now available are the additio an overhead transparency maker, a dry mount press, and an enlarged illumi nated board for viewing slides. An IBM-PC with a 512K memory, letter qu printer, and an optical scanner used for statistical analysis of tests and test scoring by the faculty is now housed in the media center.

An interesting trend in library service is the increasing number of reque from students to make copies of in-house classroom instructional programs. U their own videotapes and VCR equipment, they are able to supplement their classroom work at home, and are not limited to viewing videotapes in the library. More videotapes were placed on reserve this year then in any year the history of the library. These tapes were in-house productions of classroo programs, CAP programs, or commercially prepared tapes purchased for th library collection. Reserve videotapes were used for more than 6,000 hours during 1985-86, and the total use of all videotapes, for all purposes, was m than 6,435 hours during the academic year.

The rapidly growing multimedia collection is now housed in the new M Center of the library. Access to this collection is through the card catalog a through a microcomputer-produced title, format, and subject catalog.

Production services also have increased for the Delaware Campus Libra Media Center. Slide production (in coordination with the Pennsylvania Cam Media Center), videotape duplications and transfers from one format to ano audiotape duplications, video production for seminars and campus activities expanding rapidly. The use of the Media Center's 35mm cameras by faculty staff, and students has increased dramatically in the past year. These camer are particularly important for serving the increasing demands of the Travel Tourism programs, and those of the School of Hotel and Restaurant Managen

Over 50,000 books, as well as shelves, furniture etc., are moved to new quarters by students, faculty and staff at Brandywine College.

LAW LIBRARY

THE COLLECTION This year marked a watershed in the growth and development of the Law Library. The coalescence of four factors brought tl about: the library expansion; the AALS inspection, the personnel reorganiza and achieving a 200,000 volume count.

The library addition provided critically needed space to accomplish our ol tives: shelf space for expansion of the collection, a new computer lab, microform room, audiovisual studio, six conference rooms, staff lounge, an much needed additional seating and office space.

The AALS inspection provided the impetus for an in-house evaluation long range plan for the library. The intense effort of the library staff was rewarded by the very favorable comments of the library inspector, Betty Taylor of the University of Florida.

AUTOMATION This continues to be the area in which the greatest advances in instructional support are being made. The positive response to microcomputers and audiovisual by both students and faculty mandates that we continue the development of this area. Important applications exist for instruction, review, research, and word processing.

The new computer lab offers the students free use of Lexis and Westlaw for computer assisted legal instruction and an IBM PC with letter quality printer. The PC, in addition to word processing, is used for CALI (Computer Assisted Legal Instruction).

We are among 84 law school subscribers to CALI whose professionally prepared discs provide computer exercises using drill, simulation, tutorial, and gaming techniques for curriculum support in numerous subject areas. We expect increased usage of these discs as more faculty integrate CALI exercises in the curriculum.

This spring the computer lab was transformed into a temporary training center for Lexis instruction with nine added terminals on loan from Mead Data Central. This enabled the public services staff to provide an introductory course in Lexis to all first year students within a two week period. Additionally, training sessions in advanced research techniques were offered to faculty and upperclass students in several areas, *e.g.*, litigation and taxation. In 1986-87, a similarly designed course will be offered for Westlaw instruction.

The Pennsylvania Civil Clinic and Faculty Lounge were equipped with a Mead Data UBIQ to access Lexis bringing our total to five terminals which can be used by students and faculty. Additionally, some faculty are certified to access the Lexis and Westlaw databases through their IBM PC's. Usage of the faculty UBIQ will save on the added cost encountered by the use of the PC's.

LegalTrac and InfoTrac, our newest databases, provide up-to-date indexing of a vast number of legal and business periodicals and newspapers utilizing a combination of laser and floppy discs which are viewed on an IBM PC monitor and may be printed for future reference. Because of the multiple search capacity of this user friendly periodical index, it is replacing printed indexes where duplication occurs.

An in-house database was generated for current Delaware unreported opinions now making subject access available for these previously unindexed cases. Next year, we plan to expand the database retrospectively and develop a similar database for Delaware bills. This will provide a unique resource for compiling legislative histories.

The card catalog was phased out and replaced with a COM (Computer Output on Microfilm) Catalog which is housed in a ROM reader. Users now have convenient access to the library's holdings in four different locations.

AUDIOVISUAL These resources are used regularly for taping moot court competitions, clinical and trial courses and CLE programs. Both the Delaware and Pennsylvania Clinics were equipped with complete audio video recording systems for instructional support. The installation of fixed and remote camera units in the trial advocacy classroom reflect state-of-the-art technology.

PERSONNEL Several administrative changes occurred within the current year. Eileen Cooper rejoined the staff as associate director of the library. The newly created Public Services Department is headed by Karin Thurman who has combined experience in reference and circulation. John Maxymuk, a Drexel University graduate in library science, has joined the staff as a reference/computer specialist. Murie Peeling was appointed serials librarian and continues on the reference desk rotation. Lisa Spencer, currently working toward her MLS, is in charge of audiovisuals. Elsie Klein, her predecessor, was transferred to the Technical Processing Department. Mary Patterson became part-time library secretary in August. In April, Zibiah Warder replaced Light Soo Hoo as circulation assistant.

Our professional staff members have provided leadership roles in the local, regional and national library community. Particularly noteworthy was the ascendancy of Jacqui Paul to the presidency of the Delaware Library Association and the Law Library's role as host of the AALL Institute in July.

77860007 42 shave
          LoLo